J. Achilles

April '93

100 GREATEST
RUNNING BACKS

100 GREATEST RUNNING BACKS

Bob Carroll

Crescent Books
A Division of Crown Publishers, Inc.

Page 1: *Doc Blanchard of Army.*

Page 2: *Tony Dorsett of the Dallas Cowboys.*

Left: *Jim Brown of the Cleveland Browns sidesteps Eagles LB Ralph Heck and goes over for a TD in 1963.*

The 1989 edition published by Crescent Books, distributed by Crown Publishers, Inc. 225 Park Avenue South New York, NY 10003

Produced by Brompton Books Corp. 15 Sherwood Place Greenwich, CT 06830 USA

Printed in Hong Kong

Library of Congress Cataloging-in-Publication Data
Carroll, Bob.
  100 greatest running backs.
    p.   cm.
  Includes index.
    1. Running backs (Football)—United States—Biography.   I. Title:
One hundred greatest running backs.
GV939.A1A12   1989
796.332'092'2—dc20
[B]   89-7689
                                                             CIP

ISBN 0-517-67730-X

h g f e d c b a

Acknowledgments

The author and publisher would like to thank the following people who helped in the preparation of this book: Mike Rose, designer; Jean Martin, editor; Rita Longabucco, picture editor; and Florence Norton, indexer.

Picture Credits

Bison Picture Library: 35(top).
Brown University Sports Information: 84(bottom).
Bucknell Sports Information: 49(bottom).
Malcolm Emmons: 2, 6(left), 7(all four), 9, 11, 15(both), 18(both), 19(right), 28, 32, 33(top), 34(bottom), 36(bottom), 38(both), 39(both), 44(top), 53, 55, 64, 66(top), 67, 68, 69, 75, 79, 81(all four), 85(both), 87, 88, 89(top), 92(all four), 93(both), 94, 95(both), 96, 98(top), 103(all three), 104, 107, 110.
Harvard Sports News Bureau: 16.
Nancy Hogue: 6(right), 36(top), 46, 49(top), 72, 89(bottom), 106(both).
L-M Productions: 8, 12(top), 22(bottom), 27(bottom), 35(top), 48, 62, 63, 73(top), 97(bottom), 99(right), 108(bottom).
University of Michigan Sports Information: 74.
University of North Texas Sports Information: 47(bottom).
University of Notre Dame Sports Information Department: 27(top), 41(left).
Ohio State University Photo Archives: 23, 44(bottom).
Penn State Sports Information: 22(top).
Princeton University Sports Information: 10(top), 54(bottom).
UPI/Bettmann Newsphotos: 1, 4, 10(bottom), 12(bottom), 13, 14, 17, 19(left), 20, 21(both), 24(top), 25(both), 26, 29, 30, 31(both), 33(bottom), 34(top), 35(bottom), 37, 40, 41(right), 42, 43, 45(both), 47(top), 50(both), 51, 52, 54(top), 56, 57, 58, 59(both), 60(both), 61, 65(both), 66(bottom), 70, 71(both), 73(bottom), 76, 77, 78, 80, 82, 83(both), 86, 90(both), 91(both), 97(top), 98(bottom), 99(left), 100, 101(all three), 102, 105, 108(top), 109.
Wake Forest Sports Information: 84(top).
Yale Sports Publicity: 24(bottom).

INTRODUCTION

Why 100 *greatest* running backs? Why not 100 *best*?

Simply because 'best' denotes pure talent. For all we know, the most talented runner who ever lived was injured in practice and never played a down. 'Greatest' depends on accomplishment. All 100 represented here accomplished wondrous things on America's football fields.

The history of football is rich with outstanding runners, and everyone has his favorites. The greatest single run we ever saw was made by a 120-pound high school senior. But maybe we just *thought* it was a great run because it gave our old high school team a rare victory.

What kind of runner are we looking for? The scatback who breaks opponents' hearts with a clutch 60-yard dash in the fourth quarter? Or the plowhorse who breaks foes' backs by plunging for first downs the whole game? One expert defined a great runner as someone who turns three-yard losses into one-yard gains. That's probably true, but it doesn't help us here.

Can two people even agree on what makes a great runner? We look for speed, elusiveness, power, durability, and courage. All 100 presented here have those qualities in varying proportions, but no one knows the perfect formula. We can only identify the results of the right mix: yards, touchdowns, wins.

Most of the great runners were pro stars, but not all. Here you'll find men who were magnificent in college but not outstanding as professionals: Jay Berwanger skipped pro football for a business career; Ernie Davis was tragically prevented from playing professionally by leukemia; Hopalong Cassady was too small to match his college success. Nevertheless, the collegiate exploits of these and several others demand their inclusion. Conversely, William Andrews only blossomed as a runner once he reached the pro level.

Statistics are a useful measuring tool, but the game has changed so much over the years that it is nearly impossible to compare rushing stats from one era to another. For example, Whizzer White's 514 yards in 1940 seems unimpressive alongside Eric Dickerson's 2105 in 1984. But did you know that White played only an 11-game schedule to Dickerson's 16? That White's team lacked a strong passing attack to spread the defenses? That White shared rushing attempts with two other runners in his backfield? Or that White also played defense, meaning he was rested through part of each game? The only constant in the two records is that they both led the NFL. White was the 'best' pro runner in 1940; Dickerson the 'best' 44 years later.

Even if we interpret statistics properly, we are faced with the problem that prior to the 1930s statistics were seldom kept. In this book we've tried to present what available statistical evidence led us to rate these 100 runners as the greatest, but some of the numbers we'd like to know were never written down.

Many of the greatest runners did other things equally well. They kicked field goals, tackled, and threw passes. When it seemed worth noting for our 100 greatest, we've mentioned other skills, but we've focused on what earned each man his place in this book – his running.

Runners are bigger and faster today. So are defenders. There are those who will say that a star of the 1920s, like Paddy Driscoll who weighed only 160 pounds, could never make a pro roster today. Of course, given today's diet and strength training, a modern-day 'Driscoll' would probably weigh about 190, but that misses the point. We might just as easily say that few of today's large leather-luggers could have excelled in 1920, when a star tailback had to be able to run, pass, punt, and play defense, often for a full 60 minutes. The only valid evaluation is how

a particular runner performed under the rules and circumstances of his own time.

Obviously we haven't seen all of our 100 runners in action. For the old-timers we investigated how they were rated at the time they played. We used such evidence as All-America and All-Pro selections, the Heisman Trophy, MVP awards, records set, team wins and losses, and the testimony of contemporary coaches and media.

At the end of this book, we've ranked our 100 runners in what we perceive as their order of greatness. It was a difficult task, and we're not even certain we'd put them in exactly the same order next week. If you are a knowledgeable fan you will probably enjoy making up your own rankings as you read on.

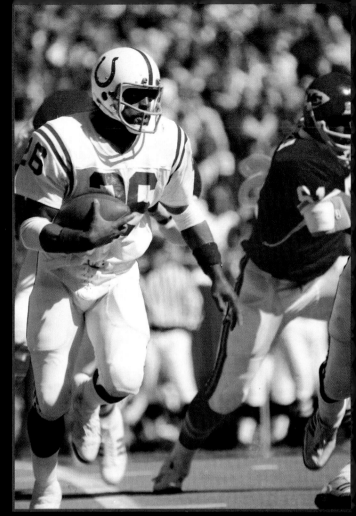

Opposite left: *Freeman McNeil.*

Opposite right: *Archie Griffin.*

Top left: *Eric Dickerson.*

Top right: *Lydell Mitchell.*

Left: *Marcus Allen.*

Above: *Franco Harris.*

Marcus Allen

Marcus Allen

The University of Southern California has produced a seemingly endless string of great tailbacks – Frank Gifford, O.J. Simpson, Mike Garrett, Charles White. In 1979, White's blocking fullback was Marcus Allen. Switched to tailback the next season, Allen began building his own legend, rushing for 1563 yards and scoring 14 touchdowns. As a senior in 1981, the 6ft 2in, 210-pound Allen rushed for 22 touchdowns and set 15 NCAA offensive records, including most yards gained rushing in a season (2342) and highest per game rushing average (212.9). He won the Heisman Trophy, the Maxwell Award, and was named to all the major All-American teams.

As the Los Angeles Raiders' first draft choice in 1982, Allen topped the NFL in touchdowns (14) and was named Rookie of the Year by *The Sporting News*. He was chosen MVP in Super Bowl XVIII when he rushed for 191 yards against Washington. Three years later he set a new record with 2314 combined rushing and receiving yards and was named NFL MVP. That year he also became the first Raider to lead the league in rushing yardage (1759).

Alan 'The Horse' Ameche

Alan Dante Ameche

Alan Ameche was a 215-pound workhorse fullback whose powerful, straight-up, head-bobbing style of running earned him his nickname. He became a regular as a freshman at the University of Wisconsin and broke the school rushing record with 824 yards. He upped that to 946 yards as a sophomore in 1952, as he led the Badgers to the Rose Bowl. Although his team lost, he gained 133 yards in the game. All-America in both his junior and senior years, he won the Heisman Trophy in 1954. The quiet, modest fullback finished his college career with 3212 yards on 673 carries for 25 touchdowns.

As a Baltimore Colts rookie in 1955, Ameche led the NFL in rushing with 961 yards and was named Rookie of the Year. He continued to provide the Colts with strong power running until his career was ended by an Achilles tendon injury in 1960. His most famous touchdown for Baltimore came in the 1958 'Sudden Death' Championship. At 8:15 of the first-ever overtime, Ameche slammed one vital yard for the winning points. His pro career totals: 4045 yards on 964 attempts and 44 TDs.

Opposite: *Marcus Allen was MVP in Super Bowl XVIII. He's still the Raiders' most consistent threat.*

Right: *Alan Ameche scored the winning TD for the Baltimore Colts in the 1958 'Sudden Death' Championship Game – the 'Greatest Game Ever Played.'*

Snake Ames

Knowlton L. Ames

Snake Ames' nickname came from his long, sinuous runs. He 'wove through a broken field like a black snake wriggles across corn stubble,' said one witness. At Princeton from 1886 to 1889, he scored 62 touchdowns (then counted at four points) by perfecting a running style that included faking, spinning, switching direction, and changing pace. An ace kicker, he added 176 PATs (two points) and 26 field goals (five points) to bring his four-year total to an amazing 730 points. He was named to the first All-America team in 1889.

Snake usually lined up as the deep man in punt formation so that he could 'read' the field before choosing his route. He was at his best when returning punts. In his greatest game – against arch-rival Harvard in 1889 – he brought a punt back 70 yards for a touchdown. He fielded his next punt below his own goal posts, ran 20 yards and slipped. Harvard's captain leaped on him, but Snake rose, shook him off and went on to score. On his third return of the day, he set up another TD with a long run.

Ottis 'O.J.' Anderson

Ottis James Anderson

Football's second 'O.J.,' Ottis James Anderson never achieved the records or the adulation of Orenthal James Simpson, and possibly the coincidence of initials (and the fact that they both wore number 32) worked against Anderson by making comparisons inevitable. Ironically, his favorite player was Gale Sayers.

He broke in with the Cardinals in 1979 with a Simpson-like game, exploding for 193 yards on 21 carries against the Dallas Cowboys. A 76-yard touchdown sprint in the final quarter proved to be the longest of his pro career. The 6ft 2in, 225-pound Miami University grad won both Rookie of the Year and NFC Player of the Year honors for his season total of 1605 rushing yards.

Although Anderson topped 1100 yards in four of his next five seasons, Cardinals fans grew increasingly impatient with the quiet, friendly star. He was criticized, perhaps unfairly, for saving his body by stepping out of bounds instead of struggling for extra yards and for putting personal accomplishments above the team's, but mostly for not being Orenthal James.

William Andrews

William Luther Andrews

At Auburn, William Andrews was known best for his blocking. Atlanta didn't draft him until the third round in 1979, but he quickly established himself, setting a Falcons record as a rookie with 1023 rushing yards. He topped 1300 yards in both 1980 and 1981. Only the strike in 1982 kept the 6ft, 213-pounder from improving his yardage again.

In 1983, when the Falcons installed the one-back offense, Andrews had his greatest season, rushing for 1567 yards. A consensus All-Pro, he was named to his fourth consecutive Pro Bowl. He repeated his 1981 feat of gaining over 2000 yards in combined rushing and passing – the second player in NFL history to do it twice. O.J. Simpson was the first.

Then a freak training camp injury in 1984 destroyed his left knee. They said he'd never play again. Andrews missed two full seasons, but after 22 months of grueling rehabilitation he returned to the Falcons to play one more season. In his final game for the Falcons, he powered a 20-6 win over Detroit with 76 yards on 18 carries. His career rushing record: 1315 attempts, 5986 yards, 4.6 average, and 30 TDs.

Opposite top: *Snake Ames, an all-time Princeton hero, 'wove through a broken field like a black snake.'*

Opposite bottom: *Cardinals RB Ottis Anderson avoids a tackler as he becomes the first rookie to rush for 100 or more yards a game in eight contests.*

Right: *Atlanta's William Andrews gained over 2000 yards rushing and receiving in two different seasons.*

Cliff Battles

Clifford Franklin Battles

Handsome Cliff Battles left little West Virginia Wesleyan College with a reputation as a Phi Beta Kappa scholar and a hell-for-leather breakaway runner. As a rookie with Boston in 1932, he led the NFL in rushing with 576 yards. The next year, in his greatest single game, he rushed for 215 yards against the New York Giants, a record that stood for 17 years.

At 6ft 1in and 195 pounds, he could hit the line with a fullback's authority, was fast enough to outrace any pursuer, and had plenty of elusive moves to get out of tight spots. Battles' heroics led his team to a division title in 1936, but Boston fans wouldn't support them. Owner George Marshall moved the team to Washington, D.C., for 1937, where Battles' running and rookie Sammy Baugh's passing took the Redskins to the 1937 Championship. Battles' 874 yards made him the first man to lead the league twice in rushing.

Cliff was 28 and in his prime. In six seasons he had rushed for 3613 yards and been named to the official All-NFL team three times. But when he asked owner Marshall for a $500 raise to $3500, he was angrily turned down and ordered to report to training camp. Equally angry, Battles retired.

Joe Bellino

Joseph Michael Bellino

In 1958-59, his first two varsity years at the Naval Academy, Joe Bellino was a good running back for a fair team. Then, in 1960, everything came together to make one of the best Navy elevens in the history of the school. Bellino was the catalyst, and his 1960 season ranks as perhaps the best ever for a Navy runner.

The Middies roared to a 9-1-0 year and were ranked fifth in the nation by the Associated Press. The 5ft 9in, 180-pound Bellino was a streaking, whirling bundle of T.N.T., as he rushed for 834 yards on 168 carries, caught 17 passes, returned punts and kick-offs, and set an Academy record with 110 points scored. Although highly-ranked Missouri finally held him in check in the Orange Bowl, he made a spectacular, diving catch to score one of Navy's TDs in the 14-21 loss. Joe's efforts earned him the Heisman Trophy, the Maxwell Award, and UPI named him College Player of the Year.

He spent four years fulfilling his obligation to the Navy, then tried pro ball with the Patriots, spending three seasons primarily as a kick returner.

Jay 'The Flying Dutchman' Berwanger

John Jacob Berwanger

Only a superlative athlete could excel for University of Chicago football teams of the 1930s. In the entire decade (before they dropped football altogether in 1939), the Maroons managed .500 seasons only three times – from 1933 to 1935. It was no coincidence that those were the three varsity years for Jay Berwanger, one of college football's greatest performers.

The 6ft 1in, 190-pound 'Flying Dutchman' was a one-man gang – running, kicking, passing, and playing linebacker on defense. In 24 games, he gained over a mile in total yardage. He was most dangerous as a runner. Against powerful Ohio State, he burst over right tackle, shook off several tacklers, and raced 85 yards for a touchdown. As so often happened, the thin Maroons eventually lost to the deep Buckeyes, but Jay's run was the play of the game. That's the story of how it went throughout his career – valiant efforts and 'moral' victories.

Berwanger, also called 'The Man in the Iron Mask' because he wore a face guard in an age when some players didn't wear helmets, received the first Heisman Trophy in 1935. Later he became the first player chosen in the NFL's first player draft, but skipped pro football to pursue a successful business career.

Opposite top: *Cliff Battles of the Boston Redskins was the first runner to lead the NFL in rushing twice.*

Opposite bottom: *Navy's Joe Bellino was the nation's top college player in 1960.*

Above: *Jay Berwanger, the first Heisman Trophy winner, carries for the University of Chicago against Michigan.*

Doc 'Mr. Inside' Blanchard

Felix Anthony Blanchard, Jr.

Nicknamed 'Little Doc' as a boy, Blanchard's first gift from his physician father was a football. It was a prophetic present. Big Doc Blanchard ranks with the top half-dozen all-time college fullbacks, and many would place him first. In three years as a consensus All-American at West Point, he never played in a losing game. Army was ranked first in the nation in 1944-45 and second in 1946. Paired with 'Mr. Outside,' spectacular breakaway speedster Glenn Davis, Blanchard was 'Mr. Inside,' so-called for his bone-crunching rumbles up the middle. Doc was sometimes stationed at flanker where his devastating blocks could spring Davis free. But the 6ft, 205-pound Blanchard had more than great strength. He possessed exceptional speed to go with his tremendous muscles and tore off numerous long runs, including a 92-yard kick-off return in his senior year.

As a junior he made a clean sweep, earning the Heisman, Maxwell, and Walter Camp awards even though Army won its games so handily that he seldom played more than a half in any contest. After graduation, he turned down numerous pro football offers, preferring to become a career Air Force officer. He retired in 1971 with the rank of Colonel.

Rocky Bleier

Robert Patrick Bleier

Rocky Bleier had few natural talents as a football player, but he became a star on four Pittsburgh Steeler Super Bowl winners by demonstrating just how far courage and will power can take a person. After an unspectacular career at Notre Dame, he wasn't drafted until the 16th round in 1968. Rocky only made the roster because of his enthusiastic special teams play, and then he was drafted into the Army before the season ended. In Vietnam he won the Bronze Star, but a grenade so injured his right foot that he was told he would be lucky to walk, much less play football. But he would not be deterred.

After extensive surgery and months of painful rehabilitation, he returned to the Steelers. In 1974, his gutsy blocking earned him a spot in the starting backfield alongside star runner Franco Harris. At first he was seldom given the ball, but on those rare occasions he showed a knack for tough yardage. More and more, he was called upon. In 1976, when he and Harris became only the second pair from the same team to gain 1000 yards in the same season, Rocky emerged as a full-fledged star. He retired after the 1980 season. His inspiring story is told in his autobiography, *Fighting Back*.

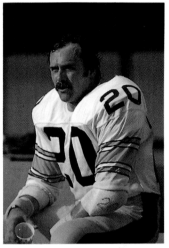

Opposite: *Army's Doc Blanchard teamed with Glenn Davis to form the most explosive 'inside-outside' punch in college football history.*

Left: *Rocky Bleier picks up some important yardage for the Steelers against the Raiders in 1975.*

Above: *After he was wounded in Vietnam, Bleier was told his football career was over, yet he came back, gaining 1000 yards in 1976.*

Charley Brickley

Charles Edward Brickley

Charley Brickley was the greatest back ever to wear Harvard's crimson. Until the 1920s, the Ivy League teams dominated college football. In both 1912 and 1913, Brickley's All-America seasons, Harvard was undefeated and regarded as the nations' leading team.

Brickley was a brilliant player in several ways, but he was such a wonderful drop-kicker – perhaps the greatest ever – that his often spectacular running is sometimes forgotten. Although he kicked 13 field goals as a sophomore in 1912, he also ran for ten touchdowns. Against Princeton, he rushed for 106 yards, a rare feat in those days. Throughout his junior year, he continued to run as well as he kicked, but the season finale against arch-rival Yale cemented his reputation as a kicker – five field goals, for all the points in a 15-5 win. The feat was all the more sensational because he suffered an eye injury during the game, which blurred his vision for the last three kicks.

An emergency appendectomy limited him to only three games in his senior year, but one of them was yet another triumph over Yale. In 1918, while serving in the Army, he was named to Walter Camp's All-Service team.

Opposite: *Jim Brown – 'the biggest cannon' – led the NFL in rushing in eight of his nine seasons. He left football to star in movies.*

Right: *Harvard's Charley Brickley was most famous for his field goal kicking, but he was a triple-threat, who could run and pass too.*

Jim Brown

James Nathaniel Brown

When a reporter asked Cleveland coach Paul Brown if he might be overusing his star fullback, the coach answered, 'When you've got the biggest cannon, you shoot it.' Jim Brown was several calibers above any other runner of his time.

In nine years (before he quit to become a movie star) he led the NFL in rushing eight times, totaled 12,312 yards, 106 rushing touchdowns, and 756 points. He set records for rushing attempts and was a marked man on every play, yet never missed a down because of injury. Special defenses were designed to stop him, but none succeeded for long. On 58 occasions he rushed for more than 100 yards in a game, topping 200 four times. His best rushing season was 1963 when he gained 1863 yards in a 14-game schedule. He was chosen Rookie of the Year in 1957, was named to nine Pro Bowls, won the Maxwell Award in 1963, and MVP in both 1958 and 1965.

Brown was the perfect combination of speed and size, a runaway boxcar at 6ft 2in and 232 pounds, with a 32-inch waist. Ironically, Cleveland had wanted to draft a quarterback in 1957, despite Brown's All-America credentials at Syracuse. When another team took the QB first, Cleveland 'settled' for Brown.

Larry Brown

Larry Brown

Larry Brown was Washington's eighth-round draft pick in 1969, the 191st player selected. At Kansas State, he had mostly blocked for other runners and, at 5ft 11in and 195 pounds, he was considered a bit small for the NFL. Worst of all, he was slow off the snap. The Redskins took a chance only because he was a 'contact' player, an aggressive hitter.

In training camp, it was discovered he had a hearing problem and could not hear the signals. Once he was fitted with a hearing aid, his slow starts disappeared and he exploded into the line with a force that made his 195 pounds seem more like 250. He led the Redskins in rushing with 880 yards as a rookie in 1969. The next year, he became the first Redskins runner ever to top 1000 yards, and his 1125 yards led the NFC. Two years later, in 1973, he hit his peak with 1216 yards, again leading the NFC.

In eight seasons, Larry rushed 1530 times for 5875 yards and 35 touchdowns. He scored 20 more TDs on pass receptions to bring his career point total to 330.

Top: *Larry Brown overcame a hearing problem to star in the NFL.*

Right: *In 1970, Brown became the first Redskins runner to top 1000 yards.*

Opposite left: *Earl Campbell poses with one of the awards he earned as 1978 rushing champion.*

Opposite right: *Campbell looks downfield for another tackler to flatten.*

Earl 'The Tyler Rose' Campbell

Earl Christian Campbell

Earl Campbell embodied raw, reckless power. The 5ft 11in, 225-pound sledgehammer used his explosive speed, heavy forearms, and barrel-like thighs to smash through tacklers like duckpins. 'He's got absolutely no regard for his body – or anybody else's body,' said his college coach Bum Phillips.

At the University of Texas he was the first player ever named All-Southwest Conference for four straight years. As a senior in 1977, he led the nation in rushing (1744 yards) and scoring (114 points on 19 touchdowns). The 'Tyler Rose' (after his Tyler, Texas, hometown) received the Heisman Trophy.

The Houston Oilers made him their number one draft choice in 1978, and he rewarded them by leading the NFL in rushing with 1450 yards while earning both Rookie of the Year and Most Valuable Player honors. In 1979 and 1980, he again led in rushing, with 1697 and 1934 yards and was twice more MVP. In 1980, he had four games with over 200 rushing yards each. After that the constant beating began to take a toll on his body and he slowed down to a mortal pace. Nevertheless, when the soft-spoken Campbell retired before the 1986 season he ranked eighth among all runners in pro football history with 9407 yards on 2187 attempts.

Tony 'The Gray Ghost of Gonzaga' Canadeo

Anthony Robert Canadeo

In 1949, Tony Canadeo of the Green Bay Packers became only the third man in NFL history to gain over 1000 yards, as he rolled up 1052 on 208 attempts during the then-12-game season. Yet, amazingly, when he graduated from high school a dozen years earlier not a single college offered him a scholarship. He finally wangled an agreement from little Gonzaga University in Washington for a scholarship if he could make the team. That was all he needed. He went on to win All-Pacific Coast and Little All-America honors. His lightning speed and a few wisps of prematurely gray hair earned him the nickname 'The Gray Ghost of Gonzaga.'

He joined the Packers in 1941 and for his first few years was used as a versatile, all-around back: running, kicking, passing, and defending. When he returned from the service after World War II, the 5ft 11in, 195-pound veteran became the Packs' heavy-duty runner, climaxing his career with his great 1949 season. During his 11 NFL seasons, he averaged 75 total yards per game in all categories. In 1974, the 'Ghost' was named to the Pro Football Hall of Fame.

Billy Cannon

William Anthony Cannon

Coach Paul Dietzel of LSU had a rule against fielding punts inside the 15-yard line. He gasped when, during the Tigers' 1959 meeting with unbeaten Mississippi, his All-America halfback Billy Cannon caught a boomer at the 11 and started upfield. A moment later, when Cannon sped 89 yards to give LSU a 7-3 victory, Dietzel was all smiles. Efforts like that took the Cannon-led Tigers to the National Championship in 1958 and earned Billy the 1959 Heisman Trophy.

No back was ever better-named. The 6ft 1in, 210-pound Cannon was no dodger; he simply exploded up the field as though shot from a howitzer. With Billy, speed plus power equaled touchdowns.

Billy joined the Houston Oilers in 1960, their first season in the fledgling American Football League, signing for $100,000. The next year he was named All-AFL as he led the league in rushing with 948 yards. The Oilers won the league championship in each of his first two seasons. A back injury threatened his career, and he was traded to the Raiders in 1964. There, he was converted to tight end and again won All-League honors for his outstanding performance.

Top: *LSU's Billy Cannon holding his 1959 Heisman Trophy.*

Right: *Cannon gains nine yards for the Oilers in the 1961 American Football League championship game.*

Opposite: *Tony Canadeo, the Packers' 'do-everything' back, returns a punt against the Redskins.*

John Cappelletti

John Raymond Cappelletti

When John Cappelletti accepted the 1973 Heisman Trophy, he dedicated it to his younger brother, Joey, who was dying of leukemia. 'If I can dedicate this trophy to him tonight and give him a couple of days of happiness,' John said, as tears streamed down his face, 'this is worth everything.'

As a youngster, John was so pigeon-toed and bow-legged that he would trip when walking, but by high school his legs had mended and he received numerous scholarship offers. He chose Penn State because it was near his home and because he was impressed with Coach Joe Paterno. In his first two seasons, he played on the defensive team, something that helped him better recognize defenses when he switched to running back. He ran for 1117 yards and 13 touchdowns as a junior, then improved to 1522 yards as a senior. He gained over 100 yards in 13 of his 22 starts, finishing as the fifth-best runner in Penn State history behind four who played at least three seasons on offense.

Cappelletti's virtues were consistency and a willingness to work hard. The 6ft 1in, 190-pounder lacked the speed to be an outstanding pro, but he put in nine seasons as a solid NFL performer.

Rick Casares

Richard José Casares

After Bronko Nagurski retired, the Chicago Bears searched for years for a fullback who could match his line-smashing. In Rick Casares they found a reasonable facsimile.

After a legendary high school career in Florida, Casares entered the University of Florida. When he cracked lines for 635 yards and seven touchdowns as a junior in 1952, he was regarded as the best fullback in the South. But after only two games as a senior, he was drafted into the service. The Bears made him their second draft choice in 1954, and when he returned he chose to play pro football.

As a rookie in 1955, the 225-pound bulldozer led the NFL in rushing yards per attempt, with 5.4. He had his greatest season in 1956, pacing the Bears to the NFL's Western Division title with a league-leading 1126 yards on 234 attempts. He scored 14 touchdowns, 12 by rushing. Casares was the kind of runner who needed only a crack in the line to barge through for a solid gain, and he could be devastating on screen passes. In a

dozen pro seasons he gained 5797 yards on 1431 attempts. He scored 49 touchdowns on the ground and 11 on pass receptions.

Opposite top: John Cappelletti of Penn State said playing defense made him a better runner.

Opposite bottom: Rick Casares of the Bears smashes for a TD against San Francisco in 1956.

Right: Hopalong Cassady scored 37 touchdowns in his four seasons at Ohio State.

Hopalong Cassady

Howard Cassady

As a freshman playing his first varsity game in 1952, Hopalong Cassady scored three touchdowns for Ohio State. Four years later, he closed out his collegiate career with another three-TD outburst in his final OSU appearance. Between those two landmarks, he carved a reputation as one of the most exciting and most consistent runners ever to play in the Big Ten.

His nickname, after a popular movie and TV cowboy of the time, was misleading; this Cassady didn't hop across a football field – he flew. He also had surprising power for a man who weighed only 172 pounds dripping wet. In four seasons, he rushed for 2466 yards on 435 attempts for a 5.7 average. His 37 touchdowns for 222 points broke Chic Harley's school record. A unanimous All-American in his junior and senior years, he led the Buckeyes to an undefeated season, a Rose Bowl victory, and a National Championship in 1954. In the crucial win over Michigan, his 61-yard run from the shadow of his goal posts launched a 99-yard drive for the winning touchdown. In 1955, 'Hoppy' rushed for 958 yards, scored 15 touchdowns, and won the Heisman, Maxwell and Camp awards.

Dutch Clark

Earl Harry Clark

Dutch Clark won All-America acclaim at tiny Colorado College, where he scored touchdowns in 21 straight games. He continued his stellar play when he joined the Portsmouth Spartans and was named All-NFL in 1931-32, his first two pro seasons.

Clark lay out the 1933 season in a money dispute, and when he returned in 1934, the Spartans had become the Detroit Lions. One thing hadn't changed – he was still All-NFL, and he remained so through 1937. He led the league in scoring in 1932, 1935, and 1936.

Although he was listed as a quarterback because he called the signals, the 6ft 1in, 180-pound triple-threat lined up at tailback in a single-wing formation. He thrived on clutch situations and was particularly dangerous running in an open field, where his uncanny balance and clever changes of pace left countless frustrated tacklers in his wake. Despite poor eyesight, he was effective as a passer and deadly as a drop-kicker.

In 1938, his final season, he earned a spot in trivia books as the last NFL player to drop-kick a field goal in an official game.

Ted Coy

Edwin Harris Coy

Ted Coy, Yale's All-America fullback of 1907-09, was the most powerful line-smasher of this century's first decade as well as an exceptional kicker. The blond bulldozer ran low to the ground with his legs driving like pistons, making him nearly unstoppable when a few precious yards were needed. In his three years, Yale lost only once.

Against Princeton in 1907, Yale trailed 10-0 when the 6ft, 195-pound Coy began carrying the ball on nearly every play. He took the team down the field on two long touchdown drives to gain the victory. The next week, he scored both of Yale's touchdowns in a 12-0 win over Harvard. Coy and Yale were strong again in 1908 but lost to Harvard on a field goal. In 1909 Ted captained the Elis, but missed the first four games due to an emergency appendectomy. By the crucial end-of-season games, he was back in form and scored all the points against Harvard as Yale capped a 10-0-0 season.

Sportswriter Grantland Rice said: 'Coy was harder to pull off his feet than a buffalo, and when he hit a tackler in the open the tackler usually took time out.'

Top: *Dutch Clark of the Detroit Lions.*

Right: *Yale immortal Ted Coy.*

Roger Craig

Roger Timothy Craig

Roger Craig is the perfect back for the San Francisco 49ers' versatile offense. An energetic, relentless, all-purpose star, he has the speed to circle the ends, the size to go up the middle, and the hands to be a reliable pass receiver. His running ability has turned innumerable short flare passes into long gains. The team rushing leader, he has also led the Niners in pass receptions three times. In 1985, he became the only player in NFL history to gain more than 1000 yards rushing and receiving in a single season, as he ran 214 times for 1050 yards and caught 92 passes for 1016. His reception total topped the NFL.

At Nebraska, Roger had only limited chances to show what he could do as a receiver. The Cornhuskers had a murderous ground attack and seldom passed. Craig rushed for 1060 yards in 1981, but played behind Heisman Trophy winner Mike Rozier in 1982. San Francisco drafted him on the second round in 1983 and he immediately became a regular, rushing for 725 yards. The next year the Niners won Super Bowl XIX, and Roger gained 135 yards rushing and receiving and scored a record three touchdowns. In Super Bowl XXIII, he caught eight passes for 101 yards and rushed 17 times for 74 yards to contribute to a 49ers victory.

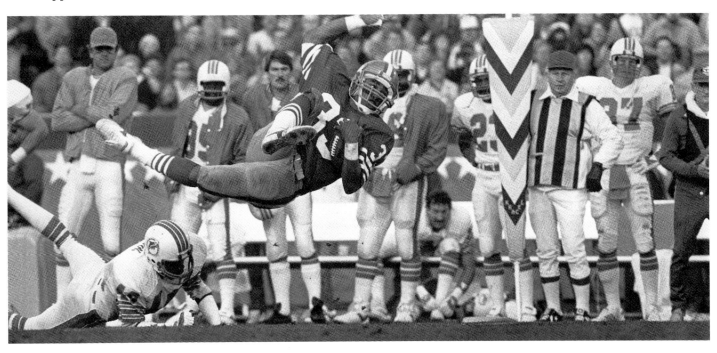

Above: *Roger Craig of the 49ers has made spectacular runs his trademark.*

Right: *Craig makes a nifty one-hand catch for a first down in Super Bowl XIX.*

John David Crow

John David Crow

John David Crow combined exceptional talent with exceptional effort to become one of the great running backs of his time. The 6ft 2in, 220-pound Louisianan was highly recruited by many colleges, but chose Texas A&M and legendary coach Bear Bryant. The Aggies were undefeated in 1956, Crow's junior year, and were ranked fifth in the nation. The following year, the team was ranked ninth by the Associated Press as Crow won the Heisman Trophy and was named to every All-America team. He rushed for 1455 yards on 296 attempts at A&M.

Chosen in the first round of the NFL draft by the Cardinals, he set a team record with an 83-yard run from scrimmage in his first pro game but spent much of his rookie year sidelined by injuries. In 1960 he rushed for 1071 yards, and in 1962 he scored 17 touchdowns, another Cardinals record. Traded to San Francisco in 1965, he played four more years, eventually switching to tight end to utilize his blocking and receiving ability. Crow completed his pro career with 4963 rushing yards on 1157 attempts. The Pro Football Hall of Fame named him to its NFL team of the 1960s.

Opposite top: *Jim Crowley was the leading rusher in Notre Dame's sensational 'Four Horsemen' backfield.*

Right: *John David Crow of Texas A & M rips through Rice on his way to the 1957 Heisman Trophy.*

Opposite bottom: *The publicity photo of the Four Horsemen.*

Jim 'Sleepy Jim' Crowley

James H. Crowley

'Outlined against a blue-gray October sky, the Four Horsemen rode again,' wrote Grantland Rice when Notre Dame defeated Army in 1924. The next day an enterprising publicity man posed Jim Crowley, Elmer Layden, Don Miller, and Harry Stuhldreher on rented horses. The photo flashed across the nation, and the Irish backfield became immortal.

The Four Horsemen were far more than a clever publicity gimmick. Each was an outstanding, multi-dimensional player, but their greatest talent was that they functioned so smoothly as a unit. Having played together since 1922, the Horsemen moved in perfect synchronization to lead Notre Dame to an undefeated season, a Rose Bowl triumph, and the 1924 National Championship. Each was named All-America.

To elevate Crowley and not the others borders on sacrilege. 'Sleepy Jim' went on to great success as a college coach, but all of the Horsemen were successful in later life. He was the heaviest at 162 pounds and was perhaps the most dangerous runner. In 1924, he led the team in scoring. In three seasons, he rushed for 1841 yards for a 6.3 average. Nevertheless, he is best considered the representative of a unique foursome, outstanding in their speed, timing, and versatility.

Larry Csonka

Lawrence Richard Csonka

Only one NFL team has ever had a perfect season – the 1972 Miami Dolphins. They roared victoriously through 14 regular-season games, two playoffs, and Super Bowl VII. If there was one irreplaceable player on that great team, he was Larry Csonka, the 6ft 3in, 235-pound fullback. Csonka's murderous up-the-gut bulldozing set up the rest of the offense. He wasn't fancy – just unstoppable – and because defenders had to concentrate on stopping Larry's smashes through the middle, they were vulnerable to quarterback Bob Griese's passes and the wide runs of Jim Kiick and Mercury Morris. The result was perfection.

At Syracuse, Csonka broke school records set by Jim Brown, Ernie Davis, Jim Nance, and Larry Little, while winning unanimous All-America honors in 1967. Miami's first-round draft choice in 1968, he gained over 1000 yards for three straight years from 1971 to 1973. He was MVP of Super Bowl VIII, rushing for 145 yards on 33 carries and scoring twice, as the Dolphins won their second championship. A five-time Pro Bowler, Csonka's career rushing totals include 8081 yards on 1891 attempts and 64 touchdowns. A powerful and durable runner, Csonka was named to the Pro Football Hall of Fame in 1987.

Ernie Davis

Ernest Davis

Ernie Davis succeeded Jim Brown as Syracuse University's premier running back. He was the ideal tailback for the Orangemen's winged-T offense. At 6ft 2in and 210 pounds, he had the size and power to smash off tackle and the speed to outdistance defenders around the end. He scored ten TDs and received some All-America mention as a sophomore in 1959. Syracuse won the National Championship, and Davis scored two touchdowns in the season-capping Cotton Bowl victory. In 1960, he was a consensus All-American, rushing for 877 yards and ten touchdowns. In 1961, Ernie became the first black to win the Heisman Trophy and was elected to every All-America team. He set Syracuse records for total yardage, points, and touchdowns, and rushed for 823 yards and 15 touchdowns.

A serious student and always cheerful, Davis was extremely popular at Syracuse and was chosen senior marshall at his graduation. Washington made him the first player chosen in the 1962 draft, but Cleveland, envisioning a powerhouse backfield of Davis and Jim Brown, traded for the right to sign him. It was not to be. While preparing for the 1962 College All-Star Game, Ernie was taken ill with leukemia. He died the following May.

Opposite: *Larry Csonka's pile-driving rushes took the Dolphins to a perfect season in 1972.*

Right: *Ernie Davis of Syracuse was the first black player to win the Heisman Trophy.*

Glenn 'Mr. Outside' Davis

Glenn Woodward Davis

Glenn Davis was 'Mr. Outside' of the most devastating one-two punch in college football history. He and fullback Doc Blanchard combined to lead Army to the National Championship in 1944 and 1945 and a number two ranking in 1946. Blazing fast, Davis was timed at ten seconds for 100 yards in a full football uniform. He also possessed a devastating change of pace, a powerful leg drive, and a strong stiff arm.

In three years, he averaged 10.1 yards every time he touched the football, and scored 59 touchdowns. He gained 944 yards rushing in 1945, but his greatest game came in 1946. With partner Blanchard slowed by injuries against Michigan, Glenn rushed for 105 yards, completed seven passes for 159 more, scored once on a 58-yard burst, threw a TD pass, intercepted two passes, and made a game-saving tackle. Coach Red Blaik called him 'the best player I have ever seen, anywhere, any time.' After finishing second two years in a row, he received the 1946 Heisman Trophy.

In 1950, after completing his Army commitment, Glenn tried pro football with the Los Angeles Rams. He led the team in rushing and scored seven touchdowns, but a recurrence of a knee injury forced his retirement the following season.

Pete Dawkins

Peter M. Dawkins

Stricken with polio in the seventh grade, Pete Dawkins underwent extensive therapy and was able to play on his junior high football team the next year. That kind of determination allowed him to brush aside predictions that he would never make the Army football team when he entered West Point in 1955. By his third year he was a regular; by his senior season he was the best player in the country.

In leading the 1958 Cadets to an 8-0-1 record, Pete rushed for 12 touchdowns and 428 yards, averaging 5.48 per carry. He caught 16 passes for 491 yards and another six TDs and returned punts and kick-offs. Army was ranked third in the polls, and Pete, a unanimous All-American, received the Heisman Trophy and Maxwell Award. *Sports Illustrated* named him Player of the Year.

Honors continued for Dawkins off the gridiron. An exceptional student, he graduated seventh in a class of

Opposite: *All-America Glenn Davis of Army.*

Above: *Davis gains 23 yards for the Rams.*

Left: *Pete Dawkins led the Cadets to an undefeated season in 1958.*

501 and was selected as a Rhodes Scholar to Oxford. He won two Bronze Stars in Vietnam, and became, at age 45, the Army's youngest general before retiring to go into an investments career.

Eric Dickerson

Eric Demitric Dickerson

Eric Dickerson is a running machine. In only five pro seasons, the 6ft 3in, 218-pound tornado moved into tenth place among all-time NFL runners. He led the league in rushing three times, including an all-time record 2105 yards in 1984, when he averaged 5.6 yards on 379 attempts. His magnificent combination of speed, size, durability, and desire makes him the most successful and highest-paid runner in football today.

In four years at Southern Methodist University, he rushed for 4450 yards on 790 attempts to break Earl Campbell's Southwest Conference records. As a senior in 1982, he won All-America honors in gaining an average of 147 yards per game and leading the Mustangs to a Cotton Bowl victory.

The Los Angeles Rams made him the second player selected in the 1983 draft. He earned NFC Rookie of the Year honors with 1808 yards on 390 attempts in his first year. He led the Rams to the playoffs in each of his first four seasons. After a contract dispute in 1987, he was sent to Indianapolis in a blockbuster trade. Although he played in only 12 games in 1987, he gained 1288 yards and took the Colts to the playoffs for the first time since 1977.

Opposite: *Eric Dickerson holds the NFL record for the most rushing yards in a season, with 2105.*

Above: *Dickerson wears goggles on the field, glasses off.*

Left: *Dickerson cuts back against the Cowboys in 1983.*

Tony Dorsett

Anthony Drew Dorsett

Left: *Tony Dorsett holds the ball high in triumph as he scores for Dallas in the 1978 NFC championship game.*

Below: *Dorsett's 2150 rushing yards as a Pitt senior earned him the 1976 Heisman Trophy.*

Tony Dorsett's achievements in four years at the University of Pittsburgh were unprecedented. Each year from 1973 to 1976, he was named to at least one major All-America team and he was virtually a unanimous choice in his final two seasons. In all four years he rushed for over 1000 yards. His greatest season was 1976, when he ran for 2150 yards and scored 134 points. Pitt won the National Championship that year, and Dorsett won the Heisman Trophy. Tony had numerous brilliant games in his college career. As a freshman, he rushed for 265 yards against Northwestern in a driving rainstorm. He gained 303 yards on 23 carries against Notre Dame in 1975. The first collegiate player to rush for over 6000 yards in his career, he finished with 6082 on 1133 attempts.

Dorsett continued to star with the Dallas Cowboys of the NFL, gaining over 1000 yards in eight different seasons. The 5ft 11in, 189-pound whiz set an NFL record with a 99-yard run on January 3, 1983, against Minnesota. He became the sixth NFL player to top 10,000 yards rushing, in 1985 against the Pittsburgh Steelers, and in 1988, his 12th pro season, he moved into second place among all-time NFL rushers.

Paddy Driscoll

John Leo Driscoll

Paddy Driscoll was the best all-around back in pro football during the 1920s. A triple-threat on offense and the best defensive back in the league, the 160-pound, former Northwestern star was most dangerous on kicks – either making them or returning them. Playing for the Cardinals in 1920, his 67-yard punt return won the Chicago City Championship for his team, an important title for the survival of the Cards. In 1923, he scored 27 points in one game; the next year, he drop-kicked a 50-yard field goal.

All-League six times, his greatest season for the Cards was 1925 when he took them to the NFL Championship. In one game he kicked four field goals to win. His most famous game occurred on Thanksgiving Day when 35,000 fans turned out to watch Red Grange in his first game for the Bears. Paddy punted 23 times, carefully placing the ball so that Grange could never make one of his famous long runs. The 0-0 tie kept the Cardinals in first place, but the fans, who had come to see Grange, booed Driscoll. It was the only time

Paddy was ever booed in Chicago. He was named to the Pro Football Hall of Fame in 1965.

Bill 'Bullet Bill' Dudley

William McGarvey Dudley

Bill Dudley was too slow, too small, threw passes sidearm and kicked with an unorthodox style. He was also a great all-around football player. Linemen ran faster, but 'Bullet Bill' was quick, shifty, and almost impossible to catch in an open field. He stood only 5ft 10in and weighed barely 170 pounds, but most of it was muscle and all of it was heart. His funny passes found their mark, and his strange place-kicks, booted without a lead-in step, creased the uprights. On defense, he was so good coaches ordered quarterbacks never to throw in his territory.

In 1941 at Virginia, Bill led the nation in scoring with 134 points and all-purpose yards with 1674. The next year he topped the NFL in rushing with 696 yards, while taking Pittsburgh to its first winning season.

During World War II, he flew missions in the Pacific but played enough football to be named to several All-Service teams. Back with the Steelers in 1946, he led the league in rushing again (604 yards), interceptions (10), and punt returns, and was named MVP. In nine pro seasons, Bill rushed for 3057 yards and had 8147 combined net yards. He was named to the Pro Football Hall of Fame in 1966.

Top: *Paddy Driscoll of the Chicago Cardinals was paid the kingly sum of $300 a game in 1920.*

Above: *Virginia's Bill Dudley received the Maxwell Award for 1942.*

Mark 'Dutchman' van Eeghen

Mark van Eeghen

Colgate University's coach introduced the wishbone offense to eastern college football in 1971 to take full advantage of sophomore Mark van Eeghen's running ability. Seldom flashy, he was a hard-charging, dependable ground-gainer. In his three seasons as a Red Raider star, van Eeghen rushed for 2591 yards on 528 attempts. As a senior in 1973, Mark ran 238 times for 1089 yards and 14 touchdowns.

The then-Oakland Raiders chose the 6ft 1in, 215-pound plowhorse on the third round in the 1974 NFL draft. He didn't become a regular until the 1975 season, but starting in 1976 he rushed for over 1000 yards for three straight seasons. In 1976, when he picked up 1012 yards on 233 attempts, the Raiders won the NFL Championship. In Super Bowl XI, Mark gained 73 yards on 18 carries to help sink the Vikings, 32-14. His top year was 1977, when he gained 1273 yards on 324 attempts, at that time a Raiders record. When the Raiders won Super Bowl XV after the 1980 season, van Eeghen drove for 80 yards on 19 carries.

In ten seasons, he gained 6651 yards on 1652 carries, retiring tied for 13th among all-time pro rushers.

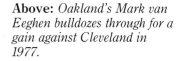

Above: *Oakland's Mark van Eeghen bulldozes through for a gain against Cleveland in 1977.*

Left: *With the Raiders for all ten of his pro seasons, the Dutchman ranks tied for 13th on the NFL's list of all-time rushers.*

Opposite: *Beattie Feathers gains eight yards for Brooklyn in 1938. Four years before, he was the first pro to rush for 1000 yards in a season.*

Beattie Feathers

William Beattie Feathers

Beattie Feathers was the first player in NFL history to rush for over 1000 yards in a single season. A brilliant single-wing tailback with terrific speed and good power, the 5ft 10in, 185-pound whirlwind started for four years for the University of Tennessee. He led the team to an undefeated record as a junior in 1932. The next year he won All-America honors and scored 13 touchdowns for the Vols. He starred in the first College All-Star Game against the Chicago Bears before the 1934 season.

After that game, he joined the Bears as a rookie.

Chicago coach George Halas put Feathers at tailback in a single-wing formation running behind the blocking of fullback Bronko Nagurski. The results were sensational. Beattie gained 1004 yards on only 101 attempts for a 9.9 average. Most of his eight touchdowns came on long runs. A shoulder injury limited him to 11 games and he missed the championship game, the only contest lost by the Bears that season. Other injuries kept Feathers from ever coming near to matching his rookie figures again. He retired after 1940 with a modest 1979 rushing yards, but for one season he was truly fantastic.

Chuck Foreman

Walter Eugene Foreman

Whether taking a hand-off or a pass, Chuck Foreman was a threat to score whenever he got the ball. His versatility keyed the attack for strong Minnesota Vikings teams in the 1970s and helped the Vikes to three Super Bowls. His quiet, almost shy, personality contrasted with his whirling, explosive running style.

Chuck set a school rushing record at the University of Miami in his junior year but was used primarily as a wide receiver as a senior. The switch ended his chance for the Heisman Trophy but helped him prepare for his all-around role with the Vikings. He started Minnesota's second game of the 1973 season and rushed for 116 yards against the Chicago Bears. The 6ft 2in, 210-pound Foreman ran for 801 yards on 182 attempts and was named NFL Rookie of the Year.

In 1975, he gained 1070 yards rushing, caught 73 passes and scored 22 touchdowns. The next season, he set the Vikings' rushing record with 1155 yards and caught 55 passes. His 1112 yards rushing in 1977 gave him three straight 1000-plus seasons. For his eight pro years, Chuck ran 1556 times for 5950 yards, caught 350 passes for 3156 yards, and scored 76 touchdowns.

Mike Garrett

Michael Lockett Garrett

Mike Garrett survived a poverty-stricken youth to become an outstanding football player. One of the great runners in USC history, Mike improved each season. As a sophomore in 1963, he rushed for 833 yards. The next year, he moved up to 948 yards. In his senior year he led the nation in rushing with 1440 yards while averaging 27 carries per game. His 3221 career rushing yards set an NCAA record at the time. He was a unanimous All-American and received the Heisman Trophy.

Although at 5ft 9in and 195 pounds he was considered rather small for pro football, Mike made the transition easily. He starred for eight years, leading his team in rushing five times. His 1087 yards in 1967 set the Kansas City team record. In 1966 he helped the Chiefs win the AFL Championship and in 1969 he paced Kansas City's Super Bowl IV winners. He completed his pro career with 5481 yards on 1308 rushing attempts.

Opposite top: *The Vikings' Chuck Foreman in action.*

Opposite bottom: *Foreman was quick and agile.*

Right: *Mike Garrett rambles through the Vikings.*

Below: *Garrett's speed and moves confounded opponents.*

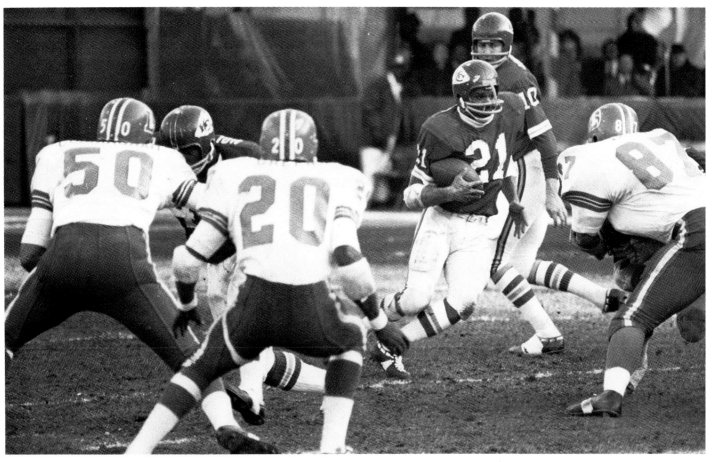

Frank Gifford

Frank Newton Gifford

Young fans know Frank Gifford as the voice of Monday Night Football, but their fathers remember him as a slashing runner and dangerous receiver for the New York Giants in the 1950s and early 1960s. Handsome and personable, he arrived in New York in 1952 with All-America credits from USC. Whether he knifed off tackle, dashed around end on a sweep, or drove downfield for a pass, the 195-pound Gifford was the key to the Giants' offense.

He was NFL Player of the Year in 1956. He rushed for 819 yards on 159 attempts, caught 51 passes for 603 yards, and scored 65 points (in a 12-game schedule) as New York won the league championship. He helped the team to division titles in 1958, 1959, 1962 and 1963.

Chosen All-NFL four times and selected to seven Pro Bowls, Frank rushed for 3609 yards on 840 attempts for a 4.3 average. After nine seasons, he retired in 1960, then returned to play three more years as a pass receiver. In 12 years, he scored 484 points, caught 367 passes, and his combined yardage was 9753. Gifford was named to the Pro Football Hall of Fame in 1977.

Left: *Before Frank Gifford became the voice of Monday Night Football, he was a Hall of Fame running back for the New York Giants.*

George 'The Gipper' Gipp

George Gipp

While on his deathbed in 1920, Notre Dame's George Gipp implored coach Knute Rockne to ask the team someday to 'win one for the Gipper.' Eight years later, Rockne repeated the story to his outmanned Irish team at halftime and inspired them to an upset victory over Army. It's one of football's most enduring legends.

Ironically, Gipp was anything but a model student at Notre Dame. He cut classes to play pool, broke all the training rules, gambled, and was known as a cynical loner. Nevertheless, he was immensely popular with his teammates, and his exceptional talents on the football field helped make Notre Dame the nation's foremost college football team.

In 1919, he led the Irish to an undefeated season, while rushing for 729 yards and passing for 727 more. In 1920, when the Irish were again undefeated, 'The Gipper' gained 332 combined yards against Army. Before he was taken fatally ill with strep throat and pneumonia near the end of the season, he rushed for 827 yards and passed for 709. As he lay dying, he learned he had become the first Notre Dame player ever to be named to Walter Camp's All-America team. He died on December 14, at age 25.

Left: *George Gipp, Notre Dame's most legendary player, helped focus national attention on the Fighting Irish.*

Above: *Generations of Notre Dame gridders have sought to 'win one for the Gipper' ever since – and usually they've succeeded.*

Biggie Goldberg

Marshall Goldberg

An unselfish star, Goldberg sacrificed personal headlines for team wins. Nicknamed 'Biggie' because he weighed only 110 pounds as a high school sophomore, Goldberg was a solid 185 in 1936 when he became regular tailback for the University of Pittsburgh. In his first game, he rushed for 208 yards on 15 carries. He gained 886 yards as a sophomore and 701 for a 6.1 average as a junior, when he was a unanimous All-American. In 1938, Pitt had other good tailbacks but no fullback. Biggie volunteered to switch to fullback where he would primarily block for others. His statistics slipped, but he scored several key touchdowns and

was again a unanimous All-American.

Before serving three years in the Navy during World War II, Goldberg was an all-purpose tailback for the weak Chicago Cardinals. The Cards built a strong team after the war, and Goldberg was penciled in as part of what was termed 'The Dream Backfield' with three other former All-Americans. But the team needed his defense more and Biggie once more went where he was needed. His work as a defensive back helped the Cardinals win the NFL Championship in 1947 and the Western Division title in 1948. He retired after the 1948 season.

Red 'The Galloping Ghost' Grange

Harold Edward Grange

Red Grange was the greatest football star of the 'Golden Age of Sports' – the 1920s. With his 1923 debut as a University of Illinois sophomore, when he scored three touchdowns and rushed for 208 yards against Nebraska, he captured the public's imagination as no player ever had before or since. Against Michigan he scored four touchdowns in the first 12 minutes on runs of 95, 67, 56, and 44 yards. The modest, 195-pound redhead had great speed, but his most effective weapon was a mystifying change of pace. All-America for three straight years, he gained 4085 yards and scored 31 TDs in only 20 games.

After playing his final game for the Illini, he turned pro with the Chicago Bears on Thanksgiving Day, 1925, and launched a 17-game nationwide tour that drew record crowds in every city. Over 70,000 stormed the Polo Grounds in New York, and 100,000 attended a game in California. His popularity made pro football a major sport for the first time. Although a knee injury in 1927 cost him much of his speed, he was still the choice at halfback when the league picked its first official All-NFL team in 1931. He retired in 1934. Grange is a charter member of the Pro Football Hall of Fame.

Archie Griffin

Archie Mason Griffin

In more than 50 years only one man has twice won the Heisman Trophy, emblematic of the nation's outstanding college football player – Archie Griffin of Ohio State, in 1974 and 1975. That alone would rank him with the greatest backs of all time, but it's only one of Griffin's accomplishments.

As a youth, he was so chubby his family nicknamed him 'Butterball,' but by 1972 he was a stocky 182-pound OSU freshman. When Coach Woody Hayes inserted him in the season's second game, he exploded for a school-record 239 rushing yards to lead a comeback victory. As a sophomore, he rushed for over 100 yards in every OSU game, a streak he continued through 31 games, an NCAA record. A three-year All-American, he gained 5177 yards on 845 carries for a 6.1 average, making him the first college player ever to rush for 5000 yards. Ohio State was 40-5-1 with Griffin in the backfield. An all-time Ohio hero, he later played eight pro seasons with Cincinnati.

Chic Harley

Charles Wesley Harley

Once upon a time, football was just another sport at Ohio State. And then came Chic Harley. In 1916-17 and 1919, with time out for World War I, his long touchdown runs and brilliant all-around play excited Buckeye fans as never before. OSU leaped to the top of the Big Ten standings and has remained a Midwest power ever since.

The 5ft 9in, 158-pound triple-threat scored 203 points in 23 OSU games. In 1916, he became the first Buckeye to be named to Walter Camp's All-America team. With Harley at halfback, State was 21-1-1, losing only his final collegiate game on a last-second Illinois field goal. Chic's sparkling touchdown dashes became legends at Columbus: 80 yards against Wisconsin, a 67-yard punt return to defeat Northwestern, four TDs against Indiana, a 40-yard scamper in State's first victory over Michigan. In only three of his starts did he fail to score.

Fans turned out in record numbers to watch Harley, expecting to be thrilled. They were seldom disappointed. After he graduated they kept coming to cheer Ohio State. Today the team plays in a huge concrete stadium built in 1922 and immediately nicknamed 'The House That Chic Built.'

Above: *Archie Griffin of Ohio State is the only player ever to have been awarded the Heisman Trophy twice.*

Left: *Chic Harley excited fans at Ohio State with his long runs in 1916-17 and 1919.*

Opposite top: *Tom Harmon leads Michigan to victory over Penn in 1939.*

Opposite bottom: *Harmon was a classic triple-threat tailback.*

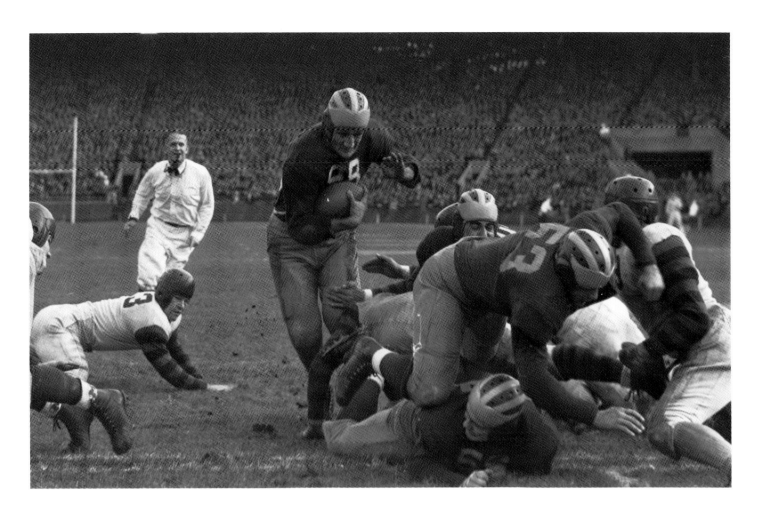

Tom 'Old 98' Harmon

Thomas D. Harmon

Tom Harmon was the most famous football player in America during the late 1930s. He even made a movie, *Harmon of Michigan*. Tailback in Michigan's powerful single-wing, the 6ft 1in, 200-pound All-American was a superb triple-threat. In three seasons for the Wolverines, he rushed for 2134 yards in 398 attempts, completed 101 of 233 passes for 1396 yards, and scored 33 touchdowns. Tom led the nation in scoring in both 1939 and 1940, totaling 237 points for his college career. His greatest individual performances included gaining 203 yards against Penn, scoring all 27 points in a win over Iowa, and 94-, 72-, and 86-yard touchdown runs against California.

He won both the Heisman Trophy and Maxwell Award in 1940 and was a first-round NFL draft choice. Instead, Tom played briefly in a short-lived rival league in 1941, then entered the Air Force. Winner of the Silver Star, he was shot down twice in enemy territory but bailed out and made his way to safety.

Although his legs were injured in the war, he played two postwar seasons with the Los Angeles Rams before retiring to pursue a successful broadcasting career. Tom passed his good looks on to his son, actor Mark Harmon.

Franco Harris

Franco Harris

At 6ft 2in and 225 pounds, Franco Harris looked like a traditional, pile-driving fullback, but he used his remarkable agility, speed, and balance to cut back for long gains like a halfback. Only when absolutely necessary did he run over a tackler – Franco preferred to dance around him or run out of bounds to avoid a hit. He knew his team needed him healthy for the next game. By running the way he did he broke off many long runs, but he was able to play 13 seasons in the NFL even though he ran the ball 2881 times, more than any man ever had before.

The Steelers' first draft choice in 1972 after only a fair career at Penn State, he gained over 1000 yards as a rookie. That fall, in the final seconds of the Steelers' first-ever playoff game, he won the game on the 'Immaculate Reception,' his shoetop catch of a deflected pass for a touchdown.

The dignified, soft-spoken Harris led Pittsburgh to four Super Bowl victories. In Super Bowl IX he rushed for 158 yards on 34 carries and was named MVP. His 12,120 rushing yards ranked third in NFL history when he retired in 1984.

Left: *Franco Harris of the Steelers was a halfback with a fullback's size. His four Super Bowl rings testify to his greatness.*

Opposite top: *Harris waves the ball in triumph after scoring Pittsburgh's fourth TD in Super Bowl XIII.*

Opposite bottom: *Abner Haynes helped popularize the American Football League in the early 1960s.*

Abner 'Butch' Haynes

Abner Haynes

Abner Haynes was the first running star of the American Football League when it set out to challenge the older NFL in 1960. His success helped pave the way for the success of the AFL, which merged with the NFL in 1970. The 6ft 1in, 198-pound Haynes ran for 1864 yards in three years at North Texas State, then chose to play pro football with the Dallas Texans of the new AFL. In 1960 he led the league in both rushing, with 875 yards, and punt returns, with a 15-yard average. He set an AFL record in 1961 with five touchdowns in one game.

Haynes' best season was his third, when he rushed for 1049 yards on 221 attempts and scored 19 touchdowns. The Texans won the championship game in two overtimes against Houston. Although Abner scored twice, he was almost the goat of the game. As team captain he called the coin toss before the first overtime; he became confused and chose to defend instead of to receive. Had Houston scored, he might never have lived down his mistake.

In eight AFL seasons, Haynes rushed for 4630 yards and gained 12,065 combined yards.

Willie Heston

William Martin Heston

More than 80 years after he hung up his football togs, Willie Heston of Michigan is still sometimes named to all-time college teams. The Wolverines were so powerful from 1901-04 that they were termed 'point-a-minute' teams. Heston was the chief point-getter. In his four seasons he scored 93 touchdowns and averaged 136 rushing yards per game. Michigan was 43-0-1. In the one tie, he ran 57 yards to set up a touchdown and then went to the sideline injured.

In 1903-04 Heston became only the second non-easterner named All-America by Walter Camp. With no passing allowed at the time, most teams tried to grind out yardage in short plunges. The 5ft 8in, 185-pound streak was a powerful runner who could move the defenders, but he was also a long-distance threat. Twice, Willie broke open games against important Michigan opponents with 75-yard touchdown runs. He was unbelievably explosive in his starts, putting him through the line before the defense could react. Once in the open, he outraced everyone to the goal line.

In 1902, Michigan played Stanford in the first Rose Bowl. Willie gained 170 yards on only 18 carries to power the 49-0 victory. Curiously, he didn't score a touchdown.

Opposite bottom: *Clarke Hinkle led the Packers to a pair of NFL championships in the 1930s.*

Right: *Willie Heston took Michigan's famed 'point-a-minute' team to the first Rose Bowl victory.*

Calvin Hill

Calvin Hill

When the Dallas Cowboys tagged Calvin Hill as their first round draft choice in 1969, many were surprised. Despite his 6ft 4in, 227-pound physique and 1512 yards rushing at Yale, his alma mater was not considered a major football power. Few Ivy League players make it in the NFL. The handsome, highly intelligent Hill was an exception. He broke the club's single-game rushing record with 138 yards in his second start. Later in that season he rushed for 150 yards in a game. He finished the 1969 season with 942 yards and Rookie of the Year honors.

The Cowboys played in Super Bowls V and VI, winning the second, but Hill suffered through injury-plagued seasons. Healthy again in 1972, he became the first Cowboy to run for 1000 yards with 1036. The next season, he set a new team record with 1142 rushing yards.

Hill joined the unsuccessful World Football League in 1975, then returned to the NFL to play six more seasons with Washington and Cleveland. In 12 NFL seasons Calvin rushed for 6083 yards on 1452 attempts and scored 390 points on 65 touchdowns. His height made him a good pass target; he caught 271 passes for 2861 yards.

Right: *Calvin Hill of Yale was one of the few modern Ivy League players to make it big in the NFL.*

Clarke Hinkle

William Clarke Hinkle

Clarke Hinkle played with a burning desire to win. At Bucknell College, he scored 128 points as a sophomore in 1929 and led undefeated teams in his final two years. During his ten years with Green Bay, the Packers won three division titles, and NFL Championships in 1936 and 1939.

Hinkle and the Chicago Bears' Bronko Nagurski were pro football's premier fullbacks during most of the 1930s, and their confrontations were legendary, as each seemed to inspire the best in the other. Not even Hinkle could match Nagurski's raw power, but the 5ft 11in, 200-pound Packer was more versatile. Clarke not only shattered lines with his power running, he could also pass, place-kick, punt, defend against passes, and back up the line with the best of them. He led the NFL in scoring with 58 points and was named All-League four times: 1936, 1937, 1938, and 1941.

Although he never led the NFL in rushing, Clarke was officially the leading career rusher in NFL history with 3850 yards when he retired after the 1941 season to enter military service. He also scored 377 points on 44 touchdowns, 29 PATs, and 28 field goals. His punting average was a sparkling 43.4.

Paul Hornung

Paul Vernon Hornung

One of Notre Dame's greatest quarterbacks, Paul Hornung won the 1956 Heisman Trophy and was Green Bay's number one draft choice in 1957. But, as the Packers' QB, he flopped dismally. When Vince Lombardi became Packers coach in 1959, he switched Hornung to halfback and the 'flop' became fabulous. Deadly on the Green Bay sweep, he was unstoppable down close to the goal line.

A good receiver and accurate kicker, Paul became a scoring machine. In his first year as a running back, he gained 681 yards and led the NFL with 94 points. In 1960, he set the all-time NFL record with 176 points. The next year he served in the Army and was only available to the Packers on weekends, yet scored 146 points. His 19 points set a championship game record as Green Bay won the title.

A handsome playboy, famous for his off-the-field exploits, Paul was suspended in 1963 for gambling on games not involving his own team, but came back strong to score 107 points in 1964. In the 1965 championship game he led the Packers to victory with 105 yards rushing. In 1986, Hornung was named to the Pro Football Hall of Fame.

Bo Jackson

Vincent E. Jackson

In all of sports history, only 24 men have played major league football and baseball in the same year. Most of them did it in the 1920s when seasons were shorter, but the most successful has been Bo Jackson, who excels today for both the Los Angeles Raiders and the Kansas City Royals.

At Auburn, where Bo also starred on both the baseball and track teams, football brought him the most headlines. In 1983, he ran for 1213 yards and was named to most All-America teams. A shoulder separation the next year caused him to miss six games. But the 6ft 2in, 222-pound Jackson came back as a senior in 1985 to gain 1786 yards, the second highest total in SEC history. He won the Heisman Trophy and was named Player of the Year by *The Sporting News*. His three-and-a-half year total of 650 rushes for 4303 yards made him Auburn's all-time leading rusher. He averaged 6.6 yards per carry and scored 43 touchdowns.

Bo signed a baseball contract with Kansas City and became a regular in 1987, hitting 20 home runs. That fall he joined the Raiders and rushed for 554 yards for a 6.8 average in only seven games.

51

John Henry 'Big John' Johnson

John Henry Johnson

Although John Henry Johnson was one of the great runners in NFL history, he was best known for his punishing blocking. Tough and durable, he put pass rushers at risk with his notorious sledgehammer elbows. Possibly no back in football history has ever protected the quarterback better than the 6ft 2in, 225-pound Johnson.

Johnson starred for St. Mary's College until they dropped football, then switched to Arizona State. Although drafted by the Pittsburgh Steelers in 1953, he played a year in Canada instead and then joined the San Francisco 49ers. All four members of the 49ers' 1954-56 backfield – Y.A. Tittle, Hugh McElhenny, Joe Perry, and Johnson – are in the Pro Football Hall of Fame. Johnson was elected in 1987.

Big John was a powerful inside runner with the speed and agility to go outside. He had strong seasons in San Francisco and helped Detroit win the 1957 NFL Championship, but his greatest years came after he was traded to Pittsburgh in 1960. He gained 1141 yards rushing in 1962 and 1048 in 1964 at age 36. In 1966, he finished his 13-season NFL career as the league's fourth-leading rusher, with 6803 yards on 1571 attempts.

Left: *John Henry Johnson dealt out punishment whether he carried the ball or blocked for a teammate.*

Left: *Ron Johnson twice rushed for over 1000 yards at Michigan and then did it twice more for the New York Giants.*

Ron Johnson

Ronald A. Johnson

Ron Johnson was a heavy-duty runner with the speed to turn a short plunge into a long gain. At the University of Michigan, he rushed for over 1000 yards in both 1967 and 1968, setting a new Big Ten rushing record as a senior with 1017 yards in conference games. He broke the NCAA single-game rushing mark, with 347 yards against Wisconsin in 1968, rushing 31 times and scoring five touchdowns.

Cleveland chose the 205-pound All-American on the first round of the 1969 draft. In his first pro season, Ron rushed for 471 yards and scored seven touch-downs but was used primarily as a blocker for Leroy Kelly. In 1970, he was traded to the Giants.

In New York, Johnson showed what he could do. He became the Giants' first 1000-yard runner with 1027, made a league-high 263 rushing attempts, caught 48 passes, and scored 12 touchdowns. In a game against Philadelphia, he broke for an 87-yard touchdown, only to have it called back on a penalty. But later, he ran 67 yards to score. Knocked out by a knee injury in 1971, he came back in 1972 to run for 1182 yards on 298 attempts with nine rushing TDs.

Charlie 'Choo-Choo' Justice

Charles Justice

In 1943 Choo-Choo Justice went from high school to the U.S. Navy. In addition to his naval duties, he played for two years with the undefeated Bainbridge Naval Training Station team; all other team members were veteran college and pro players, but Justice was the star. When Choo-Choo entered the University of North Carolina in 1946, he was already famous.

He more than lived up to his reputation. In four seasons as the North Carolina tailback, he led the Tarheels to a 32-9-1 record and three bowl appearances. Although only 5ft 10in and 176 pounds, he made up for any lack of size with his speed, agility, and versatility. Justice set a new NCAA career total offense record with 5176 yards – 3774 rushing and 2362 passing. He returned punts for 1200 yards, kick-offs for 909, and punted for a 42.5 average. In the 1950 College All-Star Game, he led the collegians to a rare victory over the pro champs and was named MVP.

Justice played briefly with the Washington Redskins in 1950 and from 1952-54. In 1953, his only full season, he rushed for 616 yards on only 115 attempts and caught 22 passes for 434 yards.

Dick 'Kaz' Kazmaier

Richard William Kazmaier, Jr.

When Dick Kazmaier was winning All-America honors at Princeton in 1950-51, football seemed in a time warp. The Tigers hadn't been a national power for years, yet Kaz led them to two consecutive perfect seasons and a pair of sixth-place rankings in the Associated Press polls. And he did it as a triple-threat tailback in an 'old-fashioned' single-wing formation. Even his size – 5ft 11in, 170 pounds – seemed to belong to a game of 25 years earlier.

But Kazmaier was a supremely gifted tailback whether running, passing, or kicking. In three years he gained 1964 yards on the ground, 2393 yards through the air, and punted for a 36.2 average. His 1827 yards in total offense led the nation in 1951. His greatest day came against a strong Cornell team in 1951, when he ran for three touchdowns and passed for three more. He totaled 360 offensive yards in the 53-15 rout.

He won nearly every important award in his senior year, taking the Heisman Trophy by the greatest margin in its 17-year history. Kaz decided against pro football and pursued a successful business career instead.

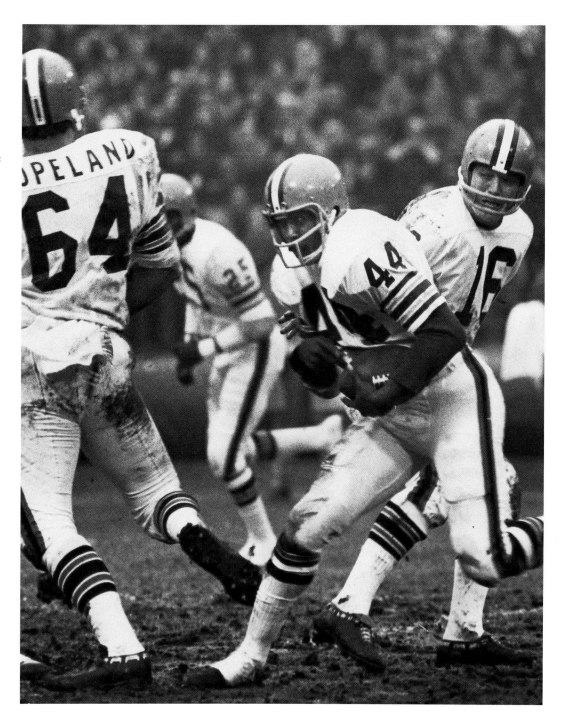

Opposite top: *Choo-Choo Justice chugged North Carolina to three bowl games in four seasons.*

Opposite bottom: *Dick Kazmaier, a single-wing tailback in the age of the T-formation, set records at Princeton and in the Heisman voting.*

Right: *Leroy Kelly kept Cleveland's running game at the top of the NFL when he replaced Jim Brown.*

Leroy Kelly

Leroy Kelly

In 1966 Leroy Kelly had perhaps the most difficult assignment ever given to a runner in NFL history – replacing Jim Brown in the Cleveland backfield. In two seasons as Brown's sub, Kelly had established himself as a fine kick returner, leading the league in punt returns in 1965, but he'd had few opportunities to run from scrimmage. Probably no back could ever make Cleveland fans forget Brown, but Kelly came as close as was humanly possible.

In his first year as a regular, the Morgan State graduate ran for 1141 yards on 209 carries. He lost the NFL rushing crown to Gale Sayers on the last day of the season. At 205 pounds, Leroy was considerably smaller than Jim Brown; he depended on a meteoric start to launch him past the line of scrimmage into the secondary where he could use his speed and shiftiness to advantage.

Kelly led the league in rushing in 1967 with 1205 yards and had his best season in 1968, with an NFL-topping 1239 yards and 16 touchdowns. Although a leg injury in 1969 reduced his speed, he had several more strong seasons. He retired after the 1973 season. His ten-year totals: 7274 yards rushing, a 4.2 average, and 74 rushing touchdowns.

John 'Jarrin' John' Kimbrough

John Alec Kimbrough

Bull-shouldered Jarrin' John Kimbrough was a prototypical line smasher. His mighty plunges in 1939 and 1940 powered Texas A&M to a 20-1 record, a pair of SWC titles, two bowl victories, and a national championship. Ten years after his final A&M season, a national poll voted him one of the three greatest fullbacks in college football history.

At 6ft 2in and 222 pounds, with his head down and knees pumping, big John was an irresistible force crashing into stacked defenses. Yet, once in the open, he ran with surprising speed and evasiveness. In 1939, as the Aggies roared to an undefeated season and national honors, he scored ten touchdowns. His greatest performance climaxed the season. In the Sugar Bowl, he rushed for 152 yards on 26 carries and scored both touchdowns in the Aggies' 14-13 win over Tulane. In 1940, he gained 611 yards rushing on 162 tries and plunged for the winning TD in a Cotton Bowl victory. In both seasons he was named to most All-America teams.

After four years of military service in World War II, the hard-charging Texan played three seasons with the Los Angeles Dons of the AAFC. He retired after the 1948 season.

Tuffy Leemans

Alphonse E. Leemans

Tuffy Leemans received little national attention as the star runner for George Washington University from 1932 to 1935 although he rushed for 2382 yards on 490 attempts. But when he won MVP honors in the 1936 College All-Star Game, he showed he was special. Nicknamed 'Tuffy' in high school when he dumped two older and larger players on their hip pads, Leemans was the first player picked by the New York Giants in the NFL's first draft.

A slashing runner, he led the NFL in rushing with 830 yards on 206 attempts as a rookie in 1936. Named All-NFL that year and again in 1939, he became a clutch performer for the Giants, starring as a rusher, receiver, passer, and defender. He even called signals from his right halfback position.

The Giants won their division three times in his eight seasons, and in 1938 took the NFL Championship. For his career, the 185-pound Tuffy rushed for 3142 yards, passed for 2324, and caught passes for another 442. He averaged better than 14 yards per punt return. The Giants retired his number 4 jersey, and in 1978 he was named to the Pro Football Hall of Fame.

Opposite: *John Kimbrough jarred loose a lot of fillings while smashing lines for Texas A & M.*

Below: *New York's Tuffy Leemans crashes for a first down against Detroit at the Polo Grounds.*

Floyd Little

Floyd Douglas Little

Floyd Little chose to attend Syracuse University because he admired Ernie Davis, and he wore Davis' number 44 with pride and distinction. At first paired with fullback Jim Nance and then with Larry Csonka, Floyd gave the Orangemen one of the best rushing attacks in America. He scored 46 touchdowns for Syracuse and gained 5529 combined yards. Little was named to various All-America teams for three straight years, from 1963-65. The Denver Broncos made him their number one draft choice in 1967.

The 5ft 10in, 196-pound Little was extremely bow-legged, yet ran with exceptional speed and balance. In nine seasons with the Broncos, he rushed for 6323 yards and 43 touchdowns on 1641 attempts and caught 215 passes for 2712 yards and nine more TDs. Floyd excelled as a kick returner, averaging 11 yards on 81 punt returns and bringing back 104 kick-offs for a 24.3 average. In 1970 he led the AFC with 901 rushing yards, and he followed this superb performance with an NFL-high 1133 in 1971.

Modest, shy and introspective, Little's outstanding play on the field and exemplary dedication to service in the community made him the Broncos' most popular player.

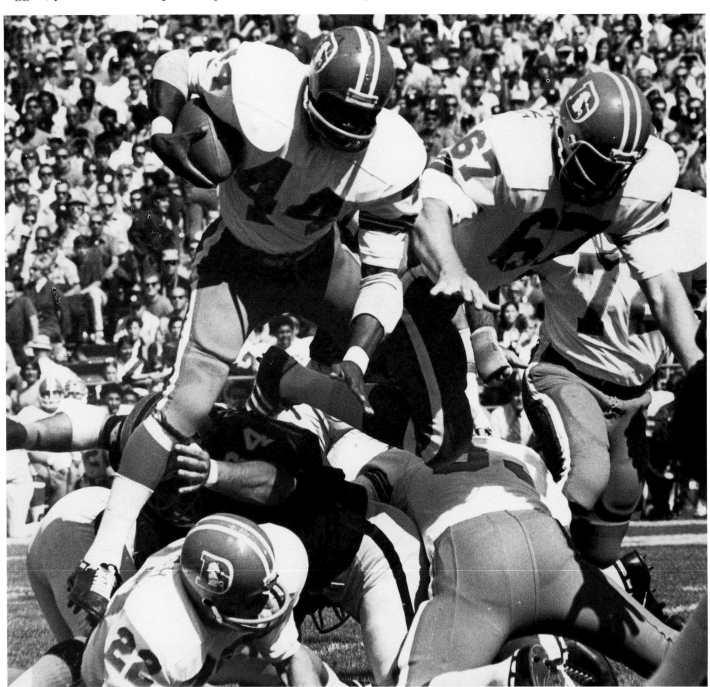

Eddie Mahan

Edward William Mahan

Eddie Mahan was a terrific breakaway runner for Harvard in the days when Ivy League schools dominated collegiate football. He joined the varsity as a sophomore in 1913 and raced 67 yards to a touchdown in his first game. His 50-yard burst helped defeat Princeton. With Charley Brickley running inside and Mahan skirting the ends, the Crimson went undefeated through nine games and won the National Championship. Both Brickley and Mahan were named All-America.

Eddie was one of the first great triple-threats. His speed and elusiveness made him a terror every time he started on an end run. Defenses usually overreacted, leaving them vulnerable to his deadly passes thrown on the run. He was also one of the top punters in the country.

Harvard was undefeated, though twice tied, in 1914. When Brickley was sidelined with appendicitis, Mahan took over his drop-kicking duties. Against arch-rival Yale, he brought an early kick back to the 27-yard line to key a 36-0 win. Eddie was named All-America again in 1914 and 1915. He captained the 8-1-0 1915 team which thumped Yale 41-0 and lost only to national champion Cornell. In Mahan's three seasons, the Crimson was 24-1-2.

Opposite: *Floyd Little was a big runner for the Broncos. Here he goes over the top against the Raiders.*

Above: *Harvard's Eddie Mahan intimidated defenses when he took off around end. In 1940, Jim Thorpe named him to his 'all-time team.'*

Right: *The Mahan-led Crimson lost only once in three years.*

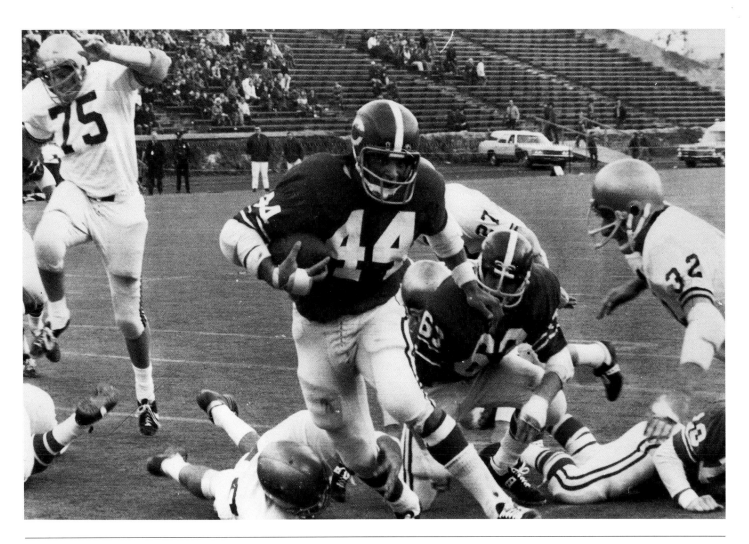

Ed Marinaro

Edward Francis Marinaro

As Sergeant Joe Coffey of TV's *Hill Street Blues*, Ed Marinaro wore a blue uniform and chased bad guys. A dozen years earlier, when he wore the red of Cornell University, opponents chased him. He was hard to catch and harder to bring down. From 1969 to 1971, big Ed set 17 NCAA records. He became the first major college back to rush for 4000 yards in three seasons, finishing his career with 4715 on 918 attempts for a 5.1 average.

As a sophomore in 1969, the 6ft 2in, 210-pound future-actor blitzed Harvard for 281 yards and five touchdowns to attract national attention. In 1971, as his 8-1-0 Cornell team tied for the Ivy League championship, Ed led the nation in rushing (1881 yards), scoring (148 points), and all-purpose running (1932 yards). He finished second in the Heisman Trophy voting.

Drafted by the Minnesota Vikings, Ed played six seasons in the NFL, rushing for 1319 yards on 383 attempts. Although he didn't duplicate his college success as a runner, his ability as a pass receiver made him a useful all-purpose back. In 1975, he rushed for 358 yards on 101 attempts and caught 54 passes for 462 yards. He ended his football career with Seattle in 1977.

Ollie Matson

Oliver Genoa Matson

One of the most remarkable athletes ever to play in the NFL, Ollie Matson was selected as a defensive All-American at San Francisco University in 1951, although he led the nation in rushing with 1566 yards. During the summer of 1952 he competed for the United States in the Olympics at Helsinki, winning the bronze medal for the 400-meter run and the silver as a member of the 1600-meter relay team. As a rookie with the Chicago Cardinals that fall, the 220-pound sprinter scored nine touchdowns, including two on kick-off returns.

After a year in the Army , he returned to the Cardi-

nals and won All-NFL honors from 1954 through 1957. In 1956, he sparked the usually bottom-dwelling Cardinals to a second place finish, as he rushed for 924 yards on 192 attempts.

Matson was traded to the Rams for nine players in 1959, running for 863 yards that fall. He later played for the Lions and Eagles. In 14 NFL seasons, Ollie rushed for 5173 yards, caught 222 passes, and scored 438 points. He tallied a record nine touchdowns on punt and kick-off returns, and totaled 12,844 combined yards. Matson was elected to the Pro Football Hall of Fame in 1972.

Opposite top: *Cornell's Ed Marinaro adds to his NCAA rushing record.*

Opposite bottom: *Marinaro in a 'football star' pose worthy of a future TV leading man.*

Above: *Ollie Matson could blast through a line, and no one could catch the Olympic*

speedster once he was in the open. Here, he dashes for a long gain against New York.

George 'One-Play' McAfee

George Anderson McAfee

At Duke, George McAfee was nicknamed 'One-Play' for his ability to score on any down. His blinding speed helped the Blue Devils go undefeated through the 1939 season. Nevertheless, Chicago Bears coach George Halas thought he had made a mistake when the spindly, 182-pound halfback showed up at training camp. All doubts vanished in McAfee's first pro game when he dashed 93 yards to a touchdown against Green Bay.

The Bears were deep in talent, and McAfee seldom played as much as a half in his first two seasons, but his long runs made him the talk of the NFL. On one sprint, he went 96 yards. In 1941, he greatest season, he carried only 65 times from scrimmage, but averaged 7.3 yards per attempt. One of the first backs to wear low-cuts, he practically danced through enemy lines, using a tricky hip swivel to break loose and his speed to out-distance pursuers.

After three years in the Navy during World War II, he scored 24 points in 17 minutes in his first game back. For eight seasons with the Bears, he averaged 12.8 yards per punt return and gained 5022 combined yards. He was elected to the Pro Football Hall of Fame in 1966.

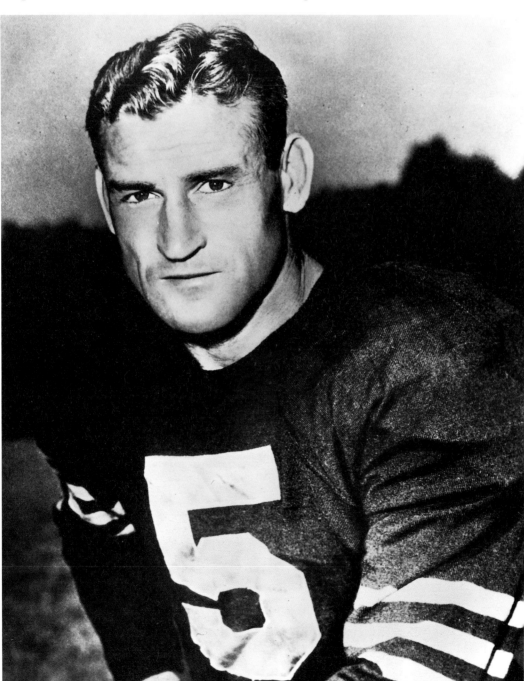

Left: *Chicago's 'One-Play' McAfee tore the NFL apart in the early 1940s with his ability to go all the way on any carry. His Bears won the 1940 Championship from Washington 73-0.*

Opposite: *McAfee was also an outstanding defender. Here, McAfee (5) helps corral a Redskin. Two other Bears Hall of Famers are tackle Jumbo Joe Stydahar (13) and guard Danny Fortmann (21).*

Lawrence McCutcheon

Lawrence McCutcheon

Low-key Lawrence McCutcheon never got the headlines of some of the flashier NFL backs, but his consistency earned him four 1000-yard seasons for the Los Angeles Rams. Only Eric Dickerson gained more career rushing yards for the Rams. The 6ft 1in, 205-pound McCutcheon was named to the Pro Bowl in half of his ten NFL seasons.

Larry's college career at Colorado State was similar to his pro seasons – excellent yardage but little national notice. Twice he topped 1000 yards, and when he finished in 1971 he had 2917 yards on 649 attempts for 22 touchdowns. The Los Angeles Rams drafted him on the third round in 1972.

After spending most of the 1972 season on the reserve squad, McCutcheon opened as a regular in 1973 and gained 120 yards in the Rams' first game. He had 21 more 100-yard regular-season games plus three in playoffs during his career. His best single game was his 202 yards against the Cardinals in the 1975 playoffs. Larry's 1000-yard seasons came in 1973, 1974, 1976, and 1977. His 1238 yards in 1978 were his personal best. When McCutcheon retired after the 1981 season, he ranked 19th among NFL runners with 6578 yards on 1521 rushing attempts.

Left: *Lawrence McCutcheon got little fanfare even though he played within spotlight-distance of Hollywood. Quietly, he rushed for over 1000 yards four times.*

Opposite top: *Hugh McElhenny spent two years in a wheelchair as a child yet became the 'king of runners.'*

Opposite bottom: *The King shows the Bears his royal stiff-arm.*

Hugh 'The King' McElhenny

Hugh Edward McElhenny

Hugh McElhenny was the king of runners during his time. No other back had his combination of speed, power, and agility. His quickness and his ability to side-step, pivot, and twist away from tacklers was all the more amazing because he was confined to a wheelchair and crutches from age nine to eleven after accidentally severing all the tendons in his left foot. At the University of Washington, he rushed for 2499 yards and was named All-America in 1951.

The 6 ft 1 in, 195-pound King was Rookie of the Year and All-NFL with the San Francisco 49ers in 1952. He scored ten touchdowns and rushed for a 7.0 average. He was off to his greatest season in 1954: After six games he had gained 515 yards on 64 attempts for an 8.0 average and scored nine TDs, but a shoulder injury ended his season. He had his personal high rushing yardage for the 49ers in 1956 with 916.

He also played for the Vikings, Giants, and Lions before retiring after the 1964 season. Hugh gained 11,375 combined yards in 13 seasons and rushed for 5281. He was elected to the Pro Football Hall of Fame in 1970.

Freeman McNeil

Freeman McNeil

Freeman McNeil 'has everything a great back should have – outstanding vision and an uncanny ability to make people miss,' says New York Jets coach Joe Walton, adding, 'When healthy, there is none better.' Unfortunately, McNeil has all too often been unhealthy. Only once has he gone through an NFL schedule without missing games – the strike-shortened 1982 season. He was in all nine games played that year and led the AFC in rushing with 786 yards on 151 attempts. But in his first seven seasons in the NFL, he missed 29 contests, more than a quarter of the Jets' schedule.

At UCLA, the 5ft 11in, 214-pound speedster set school records for rushing yards in a season, with 1396 in 1979, and for career yards, with 3195. After he was named All-America in 1980, the Jets made him their first draft choice in 1981.

Despite being sidelined at various times with a sprained foot, a separated shoulder, broken ribs, a bad ankle, and a dislocated elbow, Freeman has twice topped 1000 yards rushing in a season, with his 1331 in 1985 his personal high. He is the Jets' all-time rushing leader, with over 6000 yards.

Lydell Mitchell

Lydell Douglas Mitchell

Lydell Mitchell was a modern-style back, equally dangerous running or receiving. As a Penn State senior in 1971, he gained 1754 all-purpose yards and scored 29 touchdowns for an NCAA-record 174 points. In the Cotton Bowl he won MVP honors, rushing for 146 yards on 27 carries to lead the Nittany Lions to a 30-6 win over favored Texas.

Opposite top: *Freeman McNeil holds the Jets' all-time career rushing record.*

Opposite bottom: *On his way to a 173-yard day, McNeil zips past a baffled Dolphin.*

Below: *Baltimore's Lydell Mitchell whirls away from a pair of frustrated Lions. Three times a 1000-yard runner, he twice led the NFL in pass receiving.*

The 5 ft 11 in, 198-pound Mitchell was used sparingly as a Baltimore rookie in 1972 but blossomed in 1973 with 963 yards on 253 attempts. Meanwhile, he excelled in pass receiving. In 1974 and 1977 he led the NFL with 72 and 71 catches. In 1975 he tied for the AFC lead with 60.

Lydell became the first Colts runner to top 1000 yards in 1975, carrying 289 times for 1193 yards and 11 rushing TDs. The next year he again carried 289 times and improved his yardage to an even 1200. He made it three in a row with 1159 yards on 301 attempts in 1977. In all three of his 1000-yarders Baltimore won its division crown. Mitchell completed his nine-year pro career with 6534 rushing yards on 1675 attempts and 376 pass receptions for another 3203 yards.

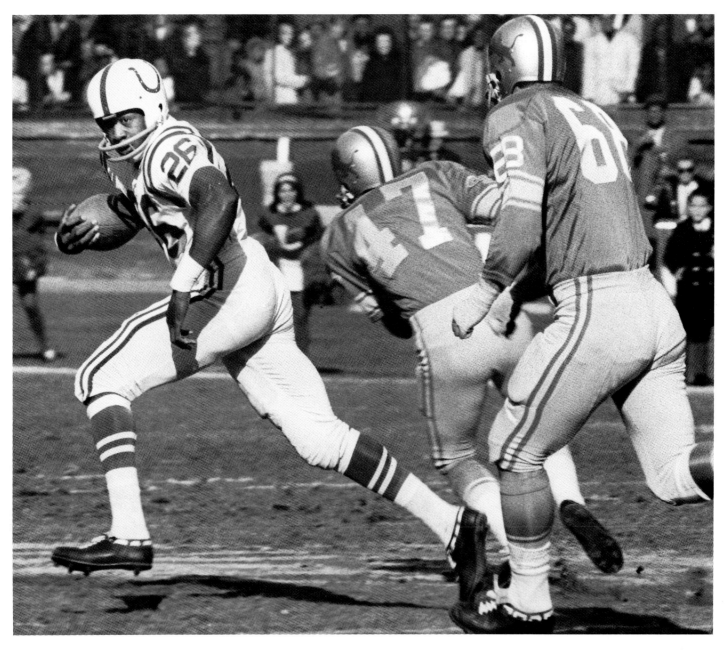

Wilbert Montgomery

Wilbert Montgomery

As a freshman at Abilene Christian University in 1973, Wilbert Montgomery scored 37 touchdowns to break Lydell Mitchell's NCAA record. Over his college career, he scored at least one TD in 32 of 35 games and rushed for 3047 yards.

A sixth-round draft choice with Philadelphia in 1977, Montgomery spent his rookie season returning kick-offs and led the NFL with a 26.9 average. One return went for 99 yards against the Giants. The next year Wilbert became the first Eagles runner to gain over 1000 yards since Steve Van Buren in 1949, rushing for 1220 yards and nine touchdowns on 259 carries. His best season was 1979, when he set team records with 338 attempts and 1512 yards. In November he ran for a career-high 197 yards against Cleveland. His 494 yards on pass receptions combined with his 1512 yards rushing made him the only NFL runner with over 2000 all-purpose yards that season.

In 1980 he was slowed by injuries but came back in time to gain 194 yards against Dallas in the playoffs to help Philadelphia to the Super Bowl. Montgomery gained 1402 yards in 1981 for his third 1000-yard season. He retired after the 1985 season with 6789 yards on 1540 attempts.

Lenny 'The Reading Comet' Moore

Leonard Edward Moore

Lenny Moore scored at least one touchdown for the Baltimore Colts in 18 straight games, from late 1963 to early in the 1965 season. One of the greatest combination runner-receivers ever to play in the NFL, Moore crossed the goal line 113 times in his 12 seasons with the Colts to earn enshrinement in the Pro Football Hall of Fame in 1975.

In three years as the leading rusher at Penn State, Lenny gained 2380 yards on only 382 attempts for a 6.2 average. Although he was named to several All-America teams in college, his greatest years were in the NFL. Rookie of the Year in 1956 when he rushed for 649 yards for a 7.5 average, he lined up as either a running back or flanker. His knifelike slashes through the line and all-out dashes around end gained him 5174 yards in his career. The 6ft 1in, 198-pound 'Reading (PA) Comet' gained another 6039 yards on 363 pass receptions.

Lenny sparked the Colts to NFL championships in 1958 and 1959. But after his injury-plagued 1963 season, many thought he was through. Instead, he rebounded with 20 touchdowns in 1964 to win Comeback of the Year honors and lead the Colts to the division title. He retired after the 1967 season.

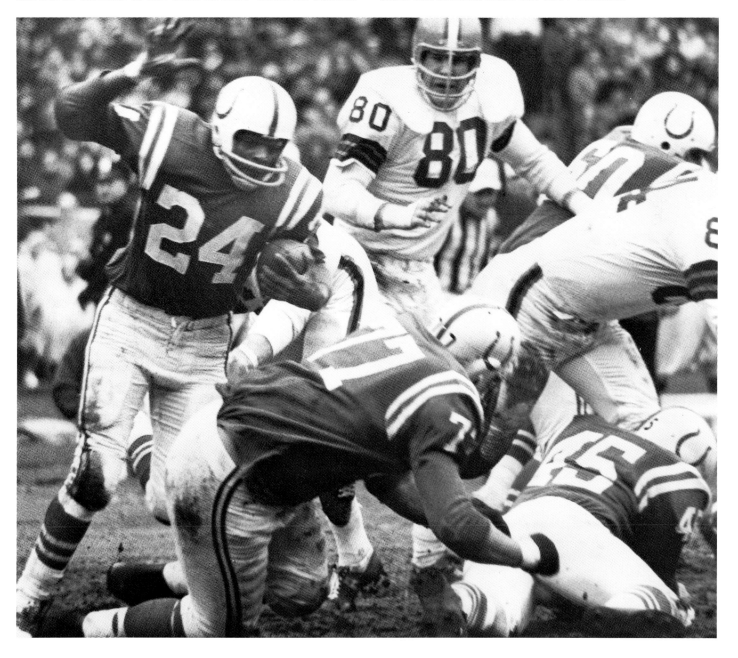

Joe Morris

Joseph Morris

It is almost an NFL rule that the name 'Joe Morris' must be preceded by the adjective 'little.' One might think the Giants' runner actually had been christened 'Little Joe.' At 5 ft 7 in, he isn't exceptionally tall, but his 195 pounds are tiny only in the behemoth world of the NFL. When he came out of Syracuse University in 1982 after an outstanding college career, most observers assumed his lack of size would limit him to a substitute's role in the pro league. In his first two seasons, that's how he was used, running the ball only 50 times from scrimmage and returning a few kick-offs.

But Giants coach Bill Parcells recognized Joe's quickness and surprising strength. In 1984, Parcells installed Morris as a backfield regular. Not coincidentally, New York jumped to second place in the NFC's Eastern Division. In 1985, Joe led New York to another second-place finish as he rushed for 1336 yards on 294 attempts to set a new Giants yardage record. His 21 rushing touchdowns was the second-highest total ever by an NFL runner.

In 1986, Joe improved his rushing record to 1516 yards on 341 attempts with 14 touchdowns, helping the Giants to go all the way that season to become Super Bowl XXI winners.

Right: *At 5ft 7in, Joe Morris is a midget in comparison to most NFL players, but his strength and quickness make him a giant for the New York Giants.*

Opposite top: *Marion Motley fights his way to a first down in the 1950 divisional playoff victory over the Giants. The win put the Browns in the championship game in their first NFL season.*

Opposite bottom: *Motley with another Browns Hall-of-Famer, quarterback Otto Graham.*

Marion Motley

Marion Motley

For four years, 1946-49, the All-America Football Conference challenged the NFL for supremacy of the pro football world. The Cleveland Browns won all four AAFC championships and so dominated the league that they hurt it by crushing competition. The Browns were merged into the NFL in 1950 and Cleveland won the title in their first year.

The Browns had many stars, but none greater than their 238-pound fullback Marion Motley. A deadly pass blocker, Motley was a terror with the ball in his huge hands. He had the speed to run away from linebackers and the power to trample them. Devastating on screen passes, his most effective play was the 'Motley Trap' up the middle; the quarterback faked a pass and slipped the ball to Motley, who exploded straight up the field, almost always for a long gain. The all-time AAFC rushing champ, Motley led the AAFC in rushing in 1948 with 964 yards and the NFL in rushing in 1950 with 810 yards. He finished his career with Pittsburgh in 1954.

In nine pro seasons, the friendly, pleasant, former University of Nevada star ran for 4720 yards for a pro-record 5.7 average. He was named to the Pro Football Hall of Fame in 1968.

Chuck Muncie

Harry Vance Muncie

Chuck Muncie's story is one of the saddest in football – that of a talented star whose career was destroyed not by injury, but by himself. An All-American at the University of California in 1975, Chuck set school career records for yards rushing (3052) and touchdowns (38). The New Orleans Saints made him the third player chosen in the 1976 NFL draft.

An immediate hit in the Saints' backfield, the 6 ft 3 in, 228-pound game-breaker became the first New Orleans runner to gain 1000 yards when he rushed for 1198 on 238 attempts in 1979. He also scored 11 TDs.

That season he was chosen MVP in the Pro Bowl.

He got off to a slow start in 1980 and his off-the-field behavior was erratic. Rumors of drug addiction began to circulate, and early in the season he was traded to San Diego for a second round draft choice. In 1981 he tied the NFL record for rushing touchdowns (19) and gained 1144 yards but he missed practices, team flights, and even games. He twice entered drug rehabilitation programs, but a final relapse in 1984 ended a career that once seemed headed for the Hall of Fame.

Bronko Nagurski

Bronislaw Nagurski

Bronko Nagurski symbolized rugged line smashing to fans in the 1930s and many eyewitnesses still insist that for sheer brutal power-running, the great Chicago Bears fullback has never been matched. Never fancy, Nagurski didn't dance, jiggle, or juke; he just plowed straight ahead, right through people. Giants center Mel Hein said: 'If you went at him at low, he would stomp you to death. If you went at him high, he just knocked you down and ran over you.'

Bronko never led the league in rushing and didn't accumulate high yardage totals by modern standards; the grind-it-out style of the 1930s didn't lend itself to large stats. His top season was 1934 when he gained 586 yards on 123 attempts. His fame stemmed from his ability to slam his 225 pounds into a stacked line and crunch through tacklers for three or four critical yards. One day he blasted across the goal line, through the end zone and into a stone wall. 'That last guy hit me awfully hard,' he admitted later.

With Bronko at his peak, the Bears won NFL championships in 1932 and 1933 and division titles in 1934 and 1937. In 1943, after a five-year retirement, he came back to help Chicago win still another championship. Asked how to stop the unstoppable Nagurski, a Giants coach answered: 'With a shotgun as he's leaving the dressing room.'

Jim Nance

James Solomon Nance

At Syracuse University from 1962 to 1964, big Jim Nance simply ran over anyone who got in his way. That style made him an excellent college fullback, but it didn't work so well for pro football when he joined the New England Patriots in 1965. Worse, his weight had ballooned to nearly 260 pounds. Instead of rolling through enemy lines, he was just roly-poly. Near the end of a disappointing season, his coach threatened to turn him into an offensive guard if he didn't cut down the calories.

One year later, at a svelte 235, Nance was a different back. He had more speed, and that improved his momentum. He began running over people again. Moreover, he had started reading defenses and using his fine cutback ability. He led the American Football League in rushing with 1458 yards on 299 attempts, both AFL records. His 11 rushing TDs also led all runners. In 1967 he carried 269 times for 1216 yards to lead the league again. Both years he was chosen All-AFL. He finished his career with the New York Jets in 1973. In eight pro seasons, the slimmed-down slammer gained 5461 yards on 1341 attempts.

Opposite: *Nagurski mauled the opposition for the University of Minnesota from 1927 to 1929.*

Left: *New England's Jim Nance increased his rushing yards by decreasing his waist line. He led the American Football League in rushing twice.*

Ernie Nevers

Ernest Alonzo Nevers

Pro football teams are named after animals, birds, colors, and even gold miners, but only one NFL team was ever named after a player – the 'Ernie Nevers Eskimos' of Duluth, Minnesota. The honor was justified. The big, blond fullback was a one-man team who ran, passed, kicked, defended, and called signals.

Pop Warner, his coach at Stanford, insisted he was better than earlier Warner great Jim Thorpe. Ernie, Pop said, had a greater competitive spirit. As a junior, Nevers suffered two broken ankles, yet came back limping to star in the Rose Bowl against Notre Dame's Four Horsemen. As a senior, he was everybody's All-American.

In 1926, he signed with Duluth of the NFL and the team was renamed in his honor. The Eskimos toured the country, playing 29 league and non-league opponents. The 200-pound Nevers played an incredible 1713 minutes of football, handling the ball on nearly every offensive play. After another tour in 1927, he took a year off to help coach Stanford. In 1929, he joined the Chicago Cardinals and played three seasons. The NFL did not keep statistics in those days, but fans, players, and coaches ranked Nevers as the best, naming him All-NFL fullback in 1930 and 1931. On Thanksgiving Day in 1929, against the Bears, he scored six touchdowns and kicked four PATs for 40 points. After 60 years, that record still stands.

Below: *Ernie Nevers of the Chicago Cardinals takes a big hit but still registers a gain.*

Opposite: *A 'one-man team,' Nevers still holds the NFL record for most points scored in a single game.*

Elmer 'Ollie' Oliphant

Elmer Quillen Oliphant

Elmer Oliphant played seven seasons of collegiate football, starring in each. He entered Purdue University in 1910, but not on a scholarship. He waited tables, carried laundry, stoked furnaces, and sold shoes to earn his way, and still found time to letter in three major sports as a sophomore, junior, and senior. In football, he helped turn Purdue from a traditional doormat into a winning team. At 5ft 8in and 178 pounds, Oliphant belied his squat build with outstanding speed and the combination of power, elusiveness and a devastating stiff-arm.

An excellent student, he received an appointment to West Point upon his graduation from Purdue. Under the eligibility rules of the time, Ollie was able to continue playing football. He was a unanimous All-American in both 1916 and 1917. His achievements included six TDs in one game, five touchdowns on runs between 50 and 96 yards in another game, and 124 points in 1917. In his four seasons, his Army team was 30-4-1 and twice undefeated. A likeable egotist, Oliphant left the Army in 1922 and later pursued a highly successful business career. Of all his many honors, he was most proud that Knute Rockne named him to his all-time All-America team.

Right: *Elmer Oliphant starred for both Purdue and Army on college gridirons. He played briefly as a professional, leading the NFL in scoring with 47 points in 1921.*

Opposite: *Walter Payton of the Bears ran more times and gained more yards than any runner in history. He was named All-NFL in six different seasons.*

Walter 'Sweetness' Payton

Walter Jerry Payton

In 13 years, Walter Payton set nearly every NFL career rushing record: most attempts (3838), most yards (16,726), most touchdowns (110), most 1000-yard seasons (10), and most 100-yard games (77). He also had the most productive single day; in 1977 he ran for 275 yards against Minnesota. His 21,053 combined yards represents almost 12 miles of offense. Yet, of all his records, his most amazing was that he played in 190 of 194 Chicago Bears games, missing one as a rookie and three because of the 1987 strike. Only 5 ft 11 in and

205 pounds, Payton established himself as the most durable runner who ever played, and certainly one of the very best.

At Jackson State University, he set a new NCAA record with 464 points scored and completed his college career with 3563 rushing yards. The Bears' first draft choice in 1975, he joined the team when it was down and struggling but was still their main running threat when Chicago won Super Bowl XX eleven years later. That season he finished second in the NFC in rushing, with 1551 yards. Several times chosen league MVP, his place in the Pro Football Hall of Fame is assured. His nickname, 'Sweetness,' referred to his running but could easily describe the cheerful, caring, and co-operative personality that made him a credit to football both on and off the field.

Don 'Perk', 'Mr. Consistent' Perkins

Donald Anthony Perkins

In his eight seasons with the Dallas Cowboys, Don Perkins earned the nickname 'Mr. Consistent.' Don made few long, breakaway runs; most of his 'big plays' were six or eight yards for needed first downs. He gained over 100 yards in only ten games but he seldom had a poor outing. He never led the NFL in rushing, but each year he finished in the top ten. From 1961 through 1968 he missed only five games, and he almost never fumbled. In one two-year stretch, he fumbled only once, on a disputed call.

After an outstanding career at the University of New Mexico, 'Perk' was slated to begin his pro career with Dallas in 1960, the team's first season. But a foot injury suffered in the College All-Star Game training camp kept him out a full year. The Cowboys, winless in their first season, were a weak team when Perkins finally joined them, but by the time 'Mr. Consistent' retired, they had become consistent winners. During his career, Don rushed 1500 times for 6217 yards and 42 touchdowns. Today, his name is one of six displayed in the 'Ring of Honor' at Texas Stadium, honoring outstanding Cowboys players of the past.

Opposite: 'Sweetness' goes over the top for a touchdown.

Left: Payton cuts downfield against the Buccaneers.

Above: Payton holds several NFL career rushing records.

Below left: Don Perkins nips through the Packers' line.

Below: Perkins follows his blocker for a Cowboys' gain.

Joe 'The Jet' Perry

Fletcher Joseph Perry

Although he had only junior college football and U.S. Navy service-ball experience, Joe Perry was an instant hit when he joined the San Francisco 49ers in 1948. At 200 pounds, he was a fullback who used speed rather than bulk to get his yardage. Quarterback Frankie Albert nicknamed him 'The Jet' because of his quick starts. He was in full stride with his first step and, once started, was difficult to catch.

Perry led the All-America Football Conference in rushing touchdowns as a rookie in 1948 and again in 1949. He also earned the 1949 rushing championship with 783 yard. When San Francisco joined the NFL, he continued to excel in the high-powered 49ers attack. With 12-game schedules in the 1950s, 1000-yard runners were rare. Perry topped the league with 1018 yards in 1953 and led again the next year with 1049 to become the first NFL runner to compile back-to-back 1000-yard seasons.

When Perry seemed to be slowing down in 1961, he was traded to Baltimore. There he had an outstanding comeback year, rushing for 675 yards. He retired after 16 seasons, a remarkably long career for a running back, having jetted for 9723 yards and 71 touchdowns on 1929 carries, all pro highs at the time.

Right: *Joe Perry breaks into the clear on a 49-yard touchdown run against the Browns.*

Opposite top: *Perry heads for the goal line in San Francisco's second NFL win.*

Opposite bottom: *Three Bears couldn't stop The Jet on this 51-yard TD sprint.*

Brian Piccolo

Louis Brian Piccolo

A successful running back needs courage – the courage to take on opponents much bigger than himself. Brian Piccolo had the courage to face the biggest opponent of all – death.

The nation's leading college rusher and scorer at Wake Forest in 1964, Brian was considered too small for pro football and no NFL team drafted him. He joined the Chicago Bears in 1966 as a substitute for roommate Gale Sayers. In 1968, Sayers was knocked out in the ninth game with a career-threatening knee injury. Piccolo took over for the last five games and carried 76 times for 269 yards, finishing with 450 yards – the best of his pro career. He worked with his friend Sayers in the off-season, helping him rehabilitate his knee.

Brian played until November of 1969 when cancer sidelined him. Sayers made a remarkable comeback to lead the NFL in rushing and at season's end was voted pro football's Most Courageous Athlete. In accepting the award, Sayers said it was Piccolo who deserved it and asked the audience to pray for Brian and 'compare his courage with that which I am supposed to possess.' Although death claimed Piccolo at age 26, he fought it till the end, and his struggle inspired millions.

Fritz Pollard

Frederick Douglas Pollard

As an All-America halfback at Brown University in 1916 and later as a pro star, Fritz Pollard was often the victim of racially-motivated, deliberately-dirty play at the bottom of pile-ups. He had the perfect answer; he went back to his position and gained more yards. Not even the most bigoted could argue that.

Fritz took his Brown team to the Rose Bowl after the 1915 season, but rain and a muddy field limited his ability to cut and change pace and the Bruins lost to undefeated Washington State. In 1916 Brown and Pollard had their greatest season. They defeated Yale on Pollard's 55-yard touchdown from scrimmage and 60-yard punt return. His long runs also sank Harvard. Walter Camp wrote: 'Pollard was the most elusive back of the year, or of any year.' The 5 ft 8 in, 150-pound Pollard was named All-America, only the second black player to be so honored.

After serving in the Army in World War I, Fritz played professionally. He led the undefeated Akron Pros to the first NFL Championship in 1920. Later he was player-coach for several teams, making him the only black ever to be a head coach in the NFL.

John 'Diesel' Riggins

John Riggins

The only predictable thing about John Riggins was that he would gain yards. A pile-driving fullback, he moved lines when he slammed into them with his powerful, 6 ft 2 in, 220-pound frame. At the University of Kansas he broke Gale Sayers' records for single-season and career yardage. While Sayers made his yards with long-distances dashes, Riggins picked up his in short but certain chunks, earning the nickname 'Diesel.' He continued his determined, durable running in the pros. In 13 seasons he rushed 2916 times for 11,352 yards and 104 touchdowns. In 1984 he set the record with 24 rushing TDs.

John's free-spirited behavior was never predictable. Haircuts were a specialty. Among his coiffures were an Afro, a Mohawk, and once a completely shaved skull. Stubborn, he sat out the entire 1980 season in a contract dispute. Reporters usually found him good for a controversial quote while his team's PR man cringed.

In Super Bowl XVII, he ran 38 times for 166 yards, but his Redskins trailed Miami 17-13 in the fourth quarter with fourth-and-one at the 43. They handed the ball to the Diesel. He slanted off left end for the first down and kept running – 43 yards to put the 'Skins ahead for good. Naturally, he was the game's MVP.

Opposite top: *Brian Piccolo's story,* Brian's Song, *stirred the hearts of the nation, both as a book and a movie.*

Opposite bottom: *Fritz Pollard led Brown University to the first Rose Bowl and the Akron Pros to the first NFL Championship.*

Top: *Washington's John Riggins in action against the Jets.*

Right: *The Diesel powers past the Cardinals.*

Gerald Riggs

Gerald Antonio Riggs

Gerald Riggs averaged six yards per rushing attempt as a senior at Arizona State to catch the Atlanta Falcons' eye. The ninth player chosen in the 1982 draft (one pick ahead of Marcus Allen), the 6ft 1in, 230-pound Riggs played sparingly in his first two seasons behind star William Andrews. But when Andrews went down with a knee injury in 1984 training camp, Gerald got his chance. In the season opener against New Orleans he carried 35 times for 202 yards to spark a 36-28 win. He finished the season with 1486 yards on 353 carries and 13 touchdowns. In 1985 he led the NFL with 397 carries and the NFC with 1719 yards.

Only the players' strike in 1987 kept Riggs from a fourth-straight 1000-yard season. Nevertheless, he was chosen for his fourth consecutive Pro Bowl. His rushing record is all the more significant because the Falcons have been consistent losers during the years he has been with them. He has not had the NFL's finest forward wall to clear his path, and Atlanta often has trailed and been forced to pass on most fourth-quarter downs, a time when runners for winning teams stack up yards.

Opposite: *Riggins breaks free for 43 yards and the winning TD in Super Bowl XVII. He was chosen the game's Most Valuable Player.*

Right: *Gerald Riggs' rushing has been one consistent highlight in several drab seasons for the Falcons.*

George Rogers

George Washington Rogers, Jr.

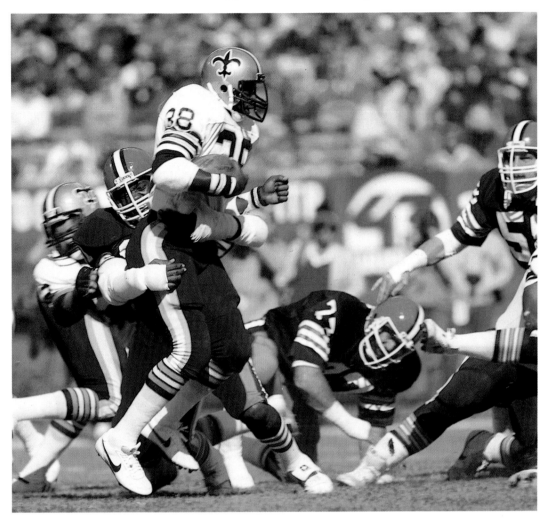

Opposite: *Gerald Riggs on the move against the 49ers.*

Left: *George Rogers of the Saints uses his power to slam through Cleveland.*

Below: *Rogers awaiting the call on the New Orleans bench. He later became the Redskins' number one runner.*

George Rogers beat the odds when he won the 1980 Heisman Trophy. His school, South Carolina, was not a big-time football giant. Still, George's record was too overpowering to be ignored. He led the nation in rushing with 1781 yards and took the Gamecocks to the greatest season in their history. Even though South Carolina lost the Gator Bowl to Pittsburgh by a one-sided, 37-9 score, Rogers was voted the game's outstanding offensive player.

The 6 ft 2 in, 224-pound Rogers made a habit of beating the odds. He overcame a poverty-stricken youth – his father was a convicted murderer – to make a life for himself. As a rookie with the New Orleans Saints in 1981, he led the NFL in rushing with 1674 yards on 378 carries. The next year, he fell victim to a drug problem, but he overcame that to have another 1000-yard season in 1983. Traded to Washington, he twice more topped the 1000-yard mark. In 1986 he carried 303 times for 1203 yards and a league-leading 18 rushing touchdowns. George's totals for his seven-year NFL career: 1692 attempts, 7176 yards, and 54 touchdowns.

Mike Rozier

Michael Rozier

Mike Rozier set an all-time NCAA record by averaging 7.16 yards per rushing attempt at the University of Nebraska. His 29 TDs in 1983 tied the NCAA record. That season, he won the Heisman Trophy by rushing for 2148 yards on 275 attempts to lead the nation. In his three years with the Cornhuskers, he ran the ball 668 times for 4780 yards and 50 touchdowns and the team posted a 33-5-0 record. The 5 ft 10 in, 198-pound Rozier had blazing speed, but also generated good power with his compact physique.

After his fantastic college record, his pro career got off to a rocky start. In 1984 he signed a reported $3.1 million contract with the first-year Pittsburgh Maulers of the springtime USFL, but was a major disappointment. So were the Maulers, who folded after one season. In 1985, with the Jacksonville Bulls, he finished a distant second to Herschel Walker in USFL rushing. With the spring league going under, he joined the NFL's Houston Oilers that fall. A combination of back-to-back seasons in one year and nagging injuries hurt him in his first two years, but his 957 yards in 11 games in 1987 indicated he had finally arrived as a pro star.

Above: *Nebraska's Mike Rozier was college football's top player in 1983 when he rushed for over 2000 yards.*

Right: *Rozier scores his first pro touchdown, going up and over for the USFL's Pittsburgh Maulers.*

Opposite left: *Chicago's Gale Sayers goes for a first down.*

Opposite right: *Sayers pulls down a pass and looks downfield.*

Gale Sayers

Gale Eugene Sayers

Gale Sayers was a comet who flashed brilliantly but all too briefly. Twice consensus All-America at Kansas, he gained even greater fame as a pro. Injuries rather than opponents finally stopped him, but for five seasons he was the most honored running back in the NFL.

Instinctively elusive and with surprising power, the 6 ft, 200-pound speedster ran with courageous abandon, a style that produced breakaway runs but put him in danger of injuries. He was 1965 Rookie of the Year with the Chicago Bears, breaking in with 22 touchdowns rushing, receiving, and returning kicks. In one game against the 49ers he scored six TDs. He started with an 80-yard pass reception, ran for scores of 1, 7, 21, and 50 yards, and finished up with an 85-yard punt return. As a sophomore in 1966 he led the NFL in rushing with 1231 yards. In 1968, after the first of several severe knee injuries, he came back to lead all runners again with 1032 yards in 1969.

Although he didn't play long enough to amass the high career totals of some, his career yardage averages are awesome – 5.0 rushing from scrimmage, 14.5 average on punt returns, and a record 30.6 mark for bringing back 91 kick-offs. He scored 56 touchdowns, all in those five brilliant seasons.

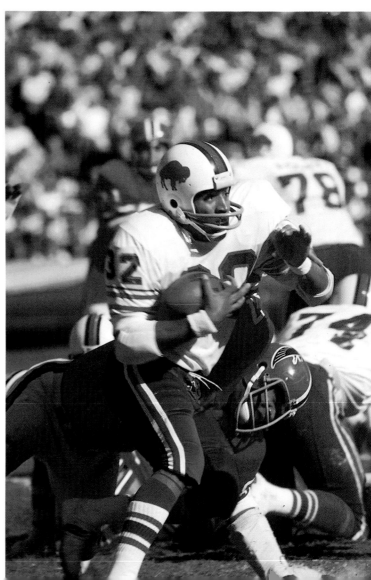

O.J. 'Juice' Simpson

Orenthal James Simpson

The most idolized running back of his generation, O.J. Simpson personified the breakaway runner. He had it all – great speed, maddening change of pace, good power, and more moves than a chess tournament. A junior college transfer to the University of Southern California in 1967, O.J. played only two years for the Trojans but was All-America both seasons. During that time he rushed for 3295 yards and 34 touchdowns in 22 games, and USC was 19-2-1. The 6ft 1in, 200-pound 'Juice' was awarded the Heisman Trophy in 1968, his senior year.

Drafted by the Buffalo Bills, Simpson's first three pro seasons were only so-so. An injury slowed him down one season, but primarily his problem was that he wasn't getting the ball enough. One Bills coach even wanted to switch him to wide receiver. When Lou Saban became Buffalo's coach in 1972, he turned Simpson loose. Simpson rushed for over 1000 yards in 1972. In 1973 he broke all pro records with 2003 yards in a 14-game season. He had one game of 250 yards and 11 over 100.

In 11 pro seasons, O.J. rushed 2404 times for 11,236 yards and 61 touchdowns. He caught 203 passes for 2142 yards and 14 more TDs. He retired after the 1979 season, and was named to the Pro Football Hall of Fame in 1985.

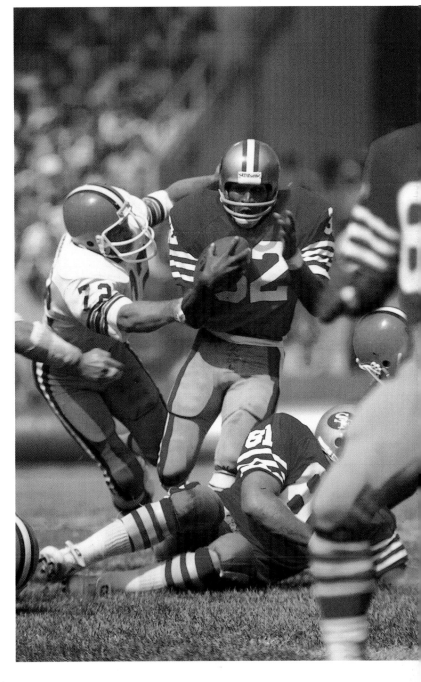

Opposite top two and bottom left: *Gale Sayers, the Bears' 'comet,' in action. In one game he scored six touchdowns.*

Opposite bottom right, above, and right: *O.J. Simpson 'juiced up' the Buffalo attack for nine seasons, and retired with the 49ers.*

Opposite: *O.J. Simpson was the 'Red Grange' of the 1970s – a superstar who packed stadiums with his famous breakaway runs.*

Left: *The Juice follows his blockers into the enemy's secondary.*

Below: *Billy Sims was the Lions' number one draft choice after he scored 42 touchdowns in two seasons at Oklahoma.*

Billy Sims

Billy Ray Sims

Despite an injury-curtailed career, Billy Sims made his mark as one of the greatest runners in history. After gaining 7738 yards in high school, he entered the University of Oklahoma. Although sidelined with injuries in 1976 and 1977, he exploded in 1978 to lead the nation in rushing with 1762 yards and in scoring with 20 touchdowns. He won the Heisman Trophy as a junior. In 1979, he ran for 1506 yards and again led in TDs with 22. Oklahoma was 20-2 with him in the lineup.

The Detroit Lions' first draft choice in 1980, he won Rookie of the Year honors by rushing for 1303 yards and 13 TDs. He lifted his rushing mark to 1437 yards and another 13 TDs as a sophomore. After the strike-shortened 1982 campaign, he came back with another 1000-yard season in 1983.

The 6 ft, 212-pound Sims ran with tremendous speed and maneuverability, yet had plenty of strength to break tackles. With the Lions he became a dangerous pass receiver, something he had seldom done at Oklahoma. Before a knee injury ended his career in mid-1984, he rushed 1131 times for 5106 yards and 42 touchdowns and caught 186 passes for 2072 yards and five TDs.

Frank Sinkwich

Francis Sinkwich

Frank Sinkwich wasn't the fastest man in the Georgia backfield. The stocky tailback ran on feet that were flatter than the gridiron, but he had 'the greatest acceleration of any back I have ever seen,' according to his coach, Wally Butts. That ability to start fast made him the nation's leading rusher in 1941 with 1103 yards on 209 attempts – the first runner to top 1000 yards in four years. In the 40-26 Orange Bowl victory over TCU, Frank gained 382 yards in total offense and scored three TDs. In 1942 he led the NCAA in total offense with 2187 yards on 795 rushing and 1392 passing. He won the Heisman Trophy and, despite sprained ankles, scored the only TD in Georgia's Rose Bowl win.

Frank entered the Marines in 1943, but his flat feet gave him a disability discharge almost immediately. He joined the Detroit Lions, and in 1944 was named NFL MVP for a great all-around season in rushing, passing, and punting. Drafted into the Army in 1945, he was injured playing service football and lost the acceleration that had made him great. After two disappointing postwar seasons, he retired.

Opposite: *Sims roars through the Packers.*

Right: *Frank Sinkwich was a triple-threat Heisman Trophy winner at Georgia.*

Below: *Versatile back Ken Strong starred for the Giants in 'The Sneakers Game,' the 1934 NFL Championship.*

Ken Strong

Elmer Kenneth Strong, Jr.

As a 1928 All-American at New York University, Ken Strong led the nation in scoring with 153 points and established himself as one of football's most versatile backs. During his long pro career, he added to his reputation. He was a dangerous runner with both power and breakaway speed, a fair passer, a superb blocker, a fine defender, and a great kicker, able to earn a living as a specialist long after a back injury ended his days as a regular. Yet the quality most often cited by teammates was his unselfish team play.

The high point of his career came in the 1934 NFL Championship. On a frozen, slippery field, his New York Giants trailed the heavily-favored Chicago Bears 10-3. At halftime, they donned basketball sneakers borrowed from Manhattan University. It took time for the Giants to get used to the traction provided by their new footwear, and the Bears added a third-quarter field goal. Then in the final quarter, New York rallied for 27 unanswered points. Strong ran 42 yards for the go-ahead touchdown and added another TD on an 11-yard scamper. Ever since, the Giants' 30-13 victory has been called 'The Sneakers Game.'

Jim Taylor

James Charles Taylor

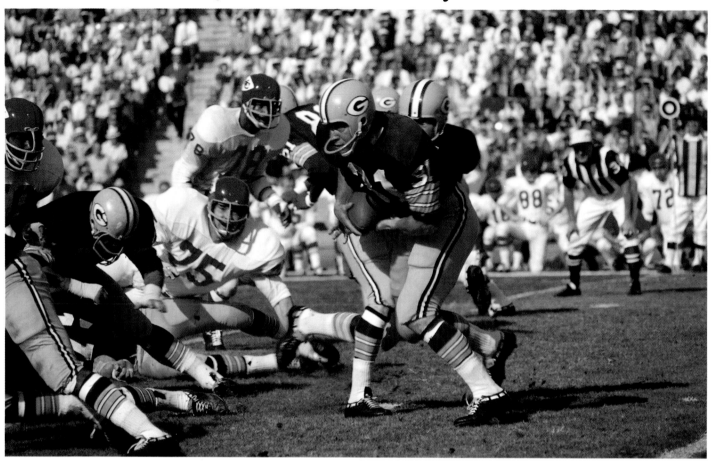

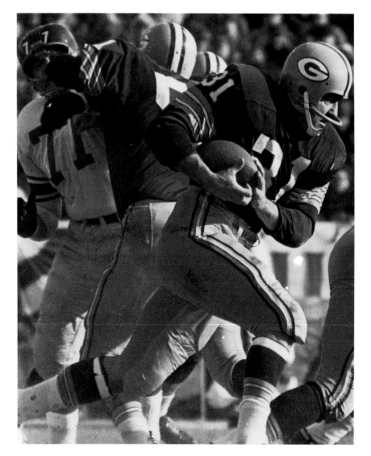

Although Jim Taylor won All-America honors at LSU in 1957, he didn't really become a great runner until he absorbed Coach Vince Lombardi's 'run to daylight' philosophy with the Green Bay Packers. A weightlifting addict, the 5 ft 11 in, 215-pound Taylor led the Packers in rushing for seven consecutive seasons, 1960-66. During that time, Green Bay won five division titles and four NFL championships, including Super Bowl I.

Taylor was a fierce blocker, adept at protecting Green Bay quarterback Bart Starr and in leading halfback Paul Hornung on the famous 'Packer Sweep.' Most of Jim's running came between the tackles. He gained over 1000 yards rushing for five straight seasons but usually trailed Cleveland's Jim Brown in yardage. In 1962 he became the only other runner to lead the NFL during Brown's nine pro seasons. That year, Jim rushed for 1474 yards on 272 attempts; he also led in scoring with 114 points on 19 touchdowns. He added a 20th TD in the championship game victory over New York, while carrying 31 times for 81 yards.

In ten NFL seasons Taylor amassed 8579 yards and 83 touchdowns on his bull-like rushes and caught passes for ten more TDs. He was named to the Pro Football Hall of Fame in 1976.

Jim Thorpe

James Francis Thorpe

Voted the greatest American athlete of the first half of the twentieth century, Jim Thorpe's accomplishments were unbelievable. A two-time All-America halfback at Carlisle Indian School, he scored 198 points in 1912. He later played seven seasons of major league baseball. In the 1912 Olympics, he won gold medals in the pentathlon and decathlon, but when it was learned that he had played minor league baseball in 1909, he was forced to return the medals. He mourned them to the day he died in 1953; in 1982, the International Olympic Committee returned them to his family.

In 1915 Thorpe accepted an offer from the Canton Bulldogs to play pro football for $250 a game. By becoming the first big-name athlete to play professionally on a regular basis, Jim raised the status of pro football. There was no organized league, but Thorpe led the Bulldogs to the unofficial pro title in 1916, 1917, and 1919. When the NFL was formed in 1920, he was elected president.

A legendary kicker, he was extraordinary in all phases of football. One of the fastest runners of his day, he hit with such power that foes accused him of wearing sheet steel in his shoulder pads. In 1963, Thorpe was among the first enshrinees in the Pro Football Hall of Fame.

Opposite top: *Jim Taylor of the Packers in Super Bowl I.*

Opposite bottom: *Taylor runs to daylight in the 1961 title game.*

Above: *Jim Thorpe – America's greatest athlete.*

Right: *Thorpe took Canton to three U.S. pro championships before the NFL was formed.*

99

Charley Trippi

Charles Louis Trippi

Charley Trippi starred for Georgia in the same backfield as 1942 Heisman Trophy winner Frank Sinkwich. When Sinkwich was hobbled for the Bulldogs' Rose Bowl game, Trippi took over and won MVP honors in the 9-0 Georgia win. Trippi was in the Air Force during World War II but returned to Georgia in 1945. He was a unanimous All-American in 1946 and won the Maxwell Award as Georgia went undefeated and won the Sugar Bowl. An extremely elusive runner, the 185-pound Trippi gained 1669 yards on 260 attempts in his Bulldog career.

Because of special wartime rules, Trippi played on four College All-Star teams, an honor normally reserved for college seniors. He joined the Chicago Cardinals in 1947 as part of their 'Dream Backfield.' In the 1947 Championship, Charley helped defeat the Eagles with touchdowns on a 44-yard run from scrimmage and a 75-yard punt return. Extremely versatile, he was the Cards' best runner for five years, then switched to T-formation quarterback for two seasons, and finished with two years as a defensive back. His rushing record showed 3506 yards on only 687 attempts for a 5.1 average. Trippi was named to the Pro Football Hall of Fame in 1968.

Opposite top: *Steve Van Buren led the Eagles to a pair of NFL titles in the 1940s.*

Right: *Charley Trippi skirts the end for six yards against the Redskins in 1947.*

Steve 'Wham-Bam' Van Buren

Steven Van Buren

A blocking back until his senior year at LSU, Steve Van Buren became the most devastating pro runner of his time. All-NFL in 1944, his rookie year with the Philadelphia Eagles, Steve led the league in punt returns and rushed for 444 yards on 80 carries for a 5.6 average. The following year, he led in rushing and kick-off returns. In a ten-game season, he scored 18 touchdowns – nearly two per game.

The 200-pound Van Buren was a 9.8 sprinter in the 100-yard dash and shifty in an open field, but he was best known as a power runner. Eagles' opponents knew he was going to smash off tackle all day, but they couldn't stop him. His dynamic line-smashing earned him the nickname 'Wham-Bam.'

In 1947 he rushed for 1008 yards and 13 TDs, the second NFL runner ever to top 1000 yards in a season. He led the Eagles to league championships in 1948 and 1949, setting a new rushing record with 1146 yards in 1949. In the championship game, he rumbled for 196 yards. Steve, who retired with the then-NFL record of 5860 rushing yards, was named to the Pro Football Hall of Fame in 1965.

Left: *Wham-Bam slams the Cards.*

Right: *Van Buren's breakaway strikes and power running made him the most unstoppable back of his day.*

101

Doak Walker

Ewell Doak Walker, Jr.

As a sophomore tailback at SMU in 1947, Doak Walker led the Mustangs to an undefeated season and was named consensus All-America. He ran for 653 yards, passed for 344 more, and set an NCAA record with his 38.7 yard kick-off return average. He followed with another outstanding season to win the Heisman Trophy as a junior. Although injured much of his senior year, he was still named to most All-America teams. When it became apparent he would again receive strong Heisman support, he asked that his name be withdrawn in favor of players who had been able to play all their games.

Many thought he would be too small (170 pounds) or too much of an all-around player for the oversized, specialized world of pro football. Instead, he confounded his critics by specializing in everything. As a Detroit Lions halfback, he was a prime pass receiver, occasional breakaway runner, place-kicker, punter, kick-returner, and emergency defensive back. He led the NFL in scoring as a rookie in 1950 with 128 points and led again with 96 in 1955, his final season. He was named to five Pro Bowls in six seasons. Perhaps Walker's most important run was a 67-yard dash for the decisive touchdown in the 1952 NFL Championship.

This page: *Herschel Walker took the Georgia Bulldogs to the National Championship as a freshman, led the USFL in rushing his rookie year with the New Jersey Generals, and joined the NFL's Dallas Cowboys in 1986.*

Opposite bottom: *Detroit's Doak Walker goes 12 yards against the 49ers in 1951. He led the Lions to victory in the 1952 NFL Championship.*

Herschel Walker

Herschel Junior Walker

When Herschel Walker scored 45 touchdowns as a high school senior, he set a national record, but he was just starting. At 222 pounds, he was a unique combination of speed and power. In 1980, his first year at the University of Georgia, he led the Bulldogs to the National Championship while rushing for 1616 yards, a new NCAA record for freshmen. He finished third in the Heisman voting. He won the award in his junior year and then left school for pro football. In three seasons at Georgia, he gained 5259 yards to rank third in NCAA history.

Herschel played three seasons, 1983-85, with the New Jersey Generals of the USFL. Although the competition was not of the same quality as the NFL, Walker's record was nonetheless remarkable. He led the league in rushing with 1812 yards in his first season, and in 1985 set new single-season professional records with 2411 yards and 438 attempts.

After the USFL folded, Walker joined the Dallas Cowboys and quickly established himself as an NFL star. Against Philadelphia in 1986, he performed the sensational feat of scoring twice on 84-yard plays, one an end run and one on a quick slant pass and dash to the end zone.

Curt Warner

Curtis Edward Warner

Curt Warner set 41 school records at Penn State. The 5ft 11in, 205-pound sprinter gained 3398 yards rushing in his four collegiate seasons. In both 1981 and 1982, his junior and senior years, he rushed for over 1000 yards. His 1982 Nittany Lions team won the National Championship by topping undefeated Georgia in the Fiesta Bowl, 27-23.

The Seattle Seahawks made Curt the third player chosen in the 1983 NFL draft, the earliest any Penn State player had ever been picked. Curt took the league by storm in his first season, rushing for an AFC-leading 1449 yards and 13 touchdowns on 335 attempts as he led the Seahawks to their first playoff.

In the opening game of 1984, Warner suffered a season-ending knee injury. It was feared he might never regain his old form. A slashing runner with speed and power, he depended on his remarkable cutback ability to break off long gains. After months of strenuous rehabilitation, he returned to the Seattle backfield in 1985 and rushed for 1094 yards. In 1986, he proved he was all the way back by again leading the AFC with 1481 rushing yards.

Kenny Washington

Kenneth S. Washington

Versatile Kenny Washington was UCLA's first All-American and one of the greatest backs ever to play on the West Coast. He first attracted national attention as a sophomore in 1937 with several long runs. In the Uclan's win over Missouri, he dashed for 87 yards to a touchdown and broke another run for 90 yards before being hauled down just short of the goal line. He continued to excel as a junior, finishing tenth in the nation in rushing. As a senior in 1939, he led the Bruins to an undefeated season.

Washington lined up at tailback in the single-wing formation, with future baseball star Jackie Robinson at wingback. Kenny's passing was nearly as effective as his running. In 1939 he led the nation in total offense, rushing 168 times for 812 yards and completing 37 of 91 passes for 582 yards. The 6ft 1in, 190-pound tailback set a UCLA career record with 3206 yards in total offense.

He played pro football for several years with minor league West Coast teams. Then in 1946, he and former UCLA teammate Woody Strode joined the Los Angeles Rams, breaking an unofficial bar against blacks that had been in effect in the NFL since 1933.

Left: *Kenny Washington broke the NFL's ban against blacks a year before his former teammate, Jackie Robinson, joined baseball's Brooklyn Dodgers.*

Opposite: *Seattle's Curt Warner topped 1000 rushing yards again in 1988 while helping the Seahawks to a division title.*

Charles White

Charles Raymond White

Charles White was one of the greatest of many outstanding University of Southern California tailbacks. He became a regular midway through his freshman season in 1976 and led the Trojans to four straight bowl games. His senior year was his best. Running from the 'I' formation, he averaged 180.3 yards per game. Against Notre Dame, he tore for 261 yards on 44 carries in leading a 44-33 win. He gained 247 yards on 39 carries and scored the winning touchdown against Ohio State in the Rose Bowl. A unanimous All-America selection, he was also awarded the Heisman Trophy for 1979.

Drafted by the Browns in 1980, he went through frustrating seasons in Cleveland. Considered by many as too small at 5 ft 10 in, 183 pounds and too slow ever to make a successful pro running back, he was also often sidelined with injuries. He missed the entire 1983 season with a broken ankle. The Browns released him in 1985, and Charles joined his old USC coach John Robinson with the Los Angeles Rams. For two seasons he subbed, but when Eric Dickerson was traded in 1987, White became the starter. In a great comeback, White led the NFL in rushing with 1374 yards on 324 attempts.

Above: *Charles White seldom got a chance to show what he could do with Cleveland.*

Left: *The Browns thought the former USC great was washed up when they released him.*

Opposite: *Rams coach John Robinson, White's former USC coach, believed in him and signed him on. In 1987, White led the NFL in rushing.*

Whizzer White

Byron Raymond White

Today, he is Justice Byron White of the United States Supreme Court, but 50 years ago, Whizzer White was one of the most exciting breakaway runners in America. As a senior at the University of Colorado in 1937, he led the nation in total offense (1596 yards), rushing (1121 yards), scoring (122 points), and all-purpose running (1970 yards) to become the Buffaloes' first All-American. Colorado was 8-0-0 through the regular season but lost to Rice in the Cotton Bowl.

Drafted number one by Pittsburgh in 1938, he signed for $15,800, making him the highest-paid player in the NFL. The 6 ft 1 in, 190-pound White led the NFL in rushing with 567 yards as a rookie, but Pittsburgh stayed at the bottom of the NFL standings. In 1939, he took a year off from football to attend Oxford University in England on a Rhodes scholarship. In the interim, Pittsburgh traded his contract to Detroit. When the Whizzer returned, he picked up where he'd left off, again leading the league in rushing with 514 yards.

After one more season with the Lions, White entered the Navy for World War II, winning two Bronze Stars. After the war, he pursued a law career that in 1962 led him to a place on the highest court in the country.

Buddy Young

Claude Young

Buddy Young was both one of the smallest and one of the biggest men in modern football history. Game programs said he was only 5 ft 4 in, but that was measured on the outside. At the University of Illinois, he tied Red Grange's one-season touchdown record, earned All-America recognition, and led the Illini to a 1947 Rose Bowl victory.

He signed with the New York Yankees of the All-America Football Conference and was an immediate star. As one of the first blacks in the AAFC, he experienced the humiliations of prejudice. When the Yankees first played in Baltimore, racists came to the stadium in blackface. Yet, when he played for Baltimore in 1953, fans voted him the most popular Colt.

Buddy packed a track star's speed, a waterbug's elusiveness and a lion's courage into his 172 pounds to outplay much bigger men. Although the teams he played for were seldom in championship contention, Buddy kept them dangerous with his long runs, especially returning kicks. In nine seasons of professional football, he averaged 27.7 yards on kick-off returns and 10.4 on punt returns.

Opposite top: *Whizzer White intercepts a Washington pass in the 1938 College All-Star Game. The All-Stars shocked the pro champs, 28-16.*

Opposite bottom: *The future Justice is flanked by two future members of the Pro Football Hall of Fame – Johnny Blood (left) and Art Rooney (right) – as he signs with Pittsburgh in 1938. Blood was the head coach and Rooney the owner.*

Right: *Buddy Young was only small on the outside. He always said he experienced more prejudice because he was short than because he was black.*

THE 100 GREATEST RUNNING BACKS

BY RANK

1. Jim Brown
2. Walter Payton
3. Red Grange
4. Jim Thorpe
5. O.J. Simpson
6. Gale Sayers
7. Steve Van Buren
8. Bronko Nagurski
9. Eric Dickerson
10. Ernie Nevers
11. Tony Dorsett
12. Earl Campbell
13. Hugh McElhenny
14. Herschel Walker
15. Joe Perry
16. Larry Csonka
17. Doc Blanchard
18. George McAfee
19. Marion Motley
20. Glenn Davis
21. Archie Griffin
22. Leroy Kelly
23. Willie Heston
24. Charley Trippi
25. Curt Warner
26. Cliff Battles
27. Billy Sims
28. Marcus Allen
29. Franco Harris
30. Jim Taylor
31. Jay Berwanger
32. Fritz Pollard
33. John Riggins
34. Ollie Matson

35. Tom Harmon
36. John Kimbrough
37. Choo-Choo Justice
38. Ted Coy
39. Hopalong Cassady
40. Lenny Moore
41. George Rogers
42. Bill Dudley
43. Floyd Little
44. Tuffy Leemans
45. Bo Jackson
46. John David Crow
47. Billy Cannon
48. Alan Ameche
49. Don Perkins
50. Snake Ames
51. Doak Walker
52. Ron Johnson
53. Ed Marinaro
54. Chuck Foreman
55. Ernie Davis
56. Dick Kazmaier
57. Eddie Mahan
58. Lydell Mitchell
59. Paddy Driscoll
60. Mike Garrett
61. William Andrews
62. Ken Strong
63. George Gipp
64. Calvin Hill
65. Gerald Riggs
66. Dutch Clark
67. Jim Nance
68. Larry Brown

69. Biggie Goldberg
70. Chuck Muncie
71. Mike Rozier
72. Frank Gifford
73. Lawrence McCutcheon
74. Kenny Washington
75. Chic Harley
76. Roger Craig
77. Clarke Hinkle
78. Ottis Anderson
79. John Henry Johnson
80. Freeman McNeil
81. Joe Morris
82. Paul Hornung
83. Pete Dawkins
84. Wilbert Montgomery
85. Abner Haynes
86. Tony Canadeo
87. Charles White
88. John Cappelletti
89. Charley Brickley
90. Elmer Oliphant
91. Whizzer White
92. Jim Crowley
93. Joe Bellino
94. Rick Casares
95. Beattie Feathers
96. Frank Sinkwich
97. Buddy Young
98. Mark van Eeghen
99. Rocky Bleier
100. Brian Piccolo

Opposite: *We can argue about the order of these 100, but most who saw him put Jim Brown at the top of the list.*

INDEX

Numerals in *italics* refer to photographs